THE HOUSE & GARDEN BOOK OF
ENGLISH GARDENS

Previous page: Gate into the vegetable garden at Barnsley House in Gloucestershire.
Above: A rose-hung tree, with the house beyond. Sutton Place, Sutton on the Forest, Yorkshire.

THE HOUSE & GARDEN BOOK OF
ENGLISH GARDENS

A PERSONAL CHOICE BY
PETER COATS
GARDEN EDITOR OF HOUSE & GARDEN

Webb&Bower
MICHAEL JOSEPH

First published in Great Britain 1988 by
Webb & Bower (Publishers) Limited
9 Colleton Crescent, Exeter, Devon EX2 4BY
in association with Michael Joseph Limited
Wright's Lane, London W8 5TZ

Designed by Steve Kibble

Production by Nick Facer/Rob Kendrew

Text and Illustrations Copyright © The Condé Nast Publications Limited 1988

British Library Cataloguing in Publication Data

Coats, Peter, *1910–*
English gardens: a personal choice.
1. Gardens————England
I. Title
712′.6′0942   SB466.G7

ISBN 0-86350-195-8

Typeset in Great Britain by Rowland Phototypesetting (London) Ltd.
Printed and bound in Hong Kong

Contents

Introduction

I must say, straight away, that this book does not contain pictures and descriptions of any of the gardens which you see in most garden books. Sissinghurst – that masterpiece of taste, probably the most beautiful garden we know, does not figure in these pages – though I have written thousands of words about it in several of the 26 garden books that I am rather surprised to find I have produced. Other omissions are the exquisite Nymans with its camellias, the prestigious Bodnant, and what I think is almost the finest garden in the world, Powis Castle. All these gardens, and we are fortunate in still having quite a few more which need, not armies (those days are past) but still a sizeable labour force, are often supported by thousands of paying visitors a year. The gardens I have included in this book are simpler, maintained by the minimum of gardeners, one or possibly two, or quite often, by the owners themselves. There are some exceptions, but that is what I have tried to make my rule: my gardens are not totally out of one's reach (over 2000 are listed in the National Gardens Scheme yellow booklet) and they are 'my sort of garden'. Egotistical, perhaps, but why not? One has one's own sort of house, one's own sort of food, one's own sort of people.

What makes my favourite sort of garden? It must look loved, not necessarily impeccably kept, but as well kept as means and time allow – in short, cared for. I love gardens with walls. At home in Scotland, I do not remember many walled gardens; ours was walled but, as in so many Scottish domains, nearly a mile away. There was a little garden round the house, but no such thing as 'French windows', as the living rooms were all on the first floor. When I came to know gardens in England, a garden one could enter directly, from the ground floor rooms, was a thing of wonder and delight.

The ideal garden, I think, should have a definite pattern, a pattern of paths, hedges, lawns and borders, but the plan should not be too rigid. An American woman friend has summed it up: 'A garden should be like a fat woman in a tight corset – bulging out of it'. Inelegantly phrased, perhaps, but apt. The plan of a garden should always be apparent, even if here and there the planting may blur it.

Colours are all-important and must be thoughtfully blended – with one exception – I do not care for one-colour borders: blue borders seem to me rather precious; yellow (or gold as they are usually called) seem brash. Borders in different reds, with apologies to my friend Peter Healing and his brave achievement shown on page 89, impress but do not absolutely move me. All white gardens are pretty, but sometimes they give me the impression that

Several important elements of an English garden in one picture: A fountain, set in silver foliage, roses (Iceberg), a glimpse of lawn and a mellow red brick wall beyond, at Mrs Diane Saunders' Easton Grey, Malmesbury, Wiltshire.

they are white, because the would-be fashionable planter did not dare to risk his or her misuse of colour. But one 'one colour' combination, when I first saw it, fairly took my heart – it was white and silver. Two colours you will say, but leaf colour can be excused, and has almost always to be there. 'Gold' flowers usually have green leaves, as do blue ones, but the silver of my white and silver garden was provided by the leaves of Pyrus salicifolia, not its flowers, and Iceberg roses. Silver and grey foliage, to my mind, are important components of the perfect garden picture, as I show on pages 115 and 116 – in the garden at Fryerning.

But, all the same, a garden should not be too studied; tall plants which belong at the back can seed themselves in the front and should be allowed to stay. The feeling of a garden is everything, but it should be light-hearted. A touch of fancy is a useful asset in any garden, like the 'cottage' conjured from a shapeless clump of old yews, and the 'W' gate, which I devised for Lord and Lady Westmorland's garden. Grandeur is not a quality I seek in my choice of gardens. The days of Kipling's terraces and 'peacocks strutting by' are past, but I have included a picture of a garden with flamingoes, and flamingoes are hardly less grand than peacocks – and they are better gardeners.

I have had a long experience of gardens, garden-planning and garden plants, so I think I am entitled to have my own very favourite gardens. As a child, I was lucky enough to be brought up in a large house (castle, actually, if one wants to show off a bit) where we had, in those more lavish days, nine gardeners, and I was allowed a garden patch all of my own, about the size of a card-table, where I grew my sort of plants and was encouraged to look after them myself – nasturtiums, lobelias, pansies, all easy to cultivate, and rewarding. Specific favourites were nemesias, with their bright colours, attractive chintzy-looking flowers. For some unknown reason, you do not often see them nowadays.

Soon after that I went to school where, too, we were encouraged to have little gardens if our own, and mine actually won a prize – which I never received. Slight disillusionment, but it fortunately had no lasting effect on my love of gardens.

Then followed a period with no opportunities to garden. This lasted

Sundrum in Ayrshire, *above*, a castle, if one wants to show off, where I was born and had my first garden. *Opposite*: Few gardens boast peacocks these days, but the enterprising Commander and Mrs Pasley Tyler have added flamingoes to the attractions of their garden at Coton House in Northamptonshire.

until my last year or so at Eton, where by chance I made friends with an ancient, but delightful, ex 'beak', Mr Luxmoore, long since retired, but who had a garden which is still there, in which I, by chance, evinced an interest. At once, Mr Luxmoore co-opted me, and allowed me to join a group of privileged boys whom he invited to relax in his garden.

We repaid his hospitality by helping him with simple, but important, garden chores, like weeding, mowing the grass, dead-heading the roses, and so on. One also had the bonus of being allowed to bathe in a fast flowing, and slightly hazardous, backwater of the Thames. Mr Luxmoore taught me much garden lore, which otherwise I might not have learned, like the legend of the Magic Brothers of the Rose, the fact that, of the five sepals of every rose flower, two have sepals which have 'whiskers' on both sides, two are 'clean shaven', and the fifth one, curiouser and curiouser, has whiskers only on one side.

This odd characteristic must have been known to the ancients, and is immortalised in a doggerel Latin poem, starting off with the lines:

Quinque sumus fratres et eodem tempore nati
Sunt duo barbati. Duo sunt sine barba creati.

This might be translated: 'We are five brothers, two of us have whiskers, two others are clean shaven', and so on. How right Walter de la Mare was: 'Through what wild centuries, roves back the rose . . .?. Something else Mr Luxmoore taught me, and is a garden trick with which to surprise your friends: do not 'grasp the nettle', but run your hand up it gently while, and this is most important, holding your breath; it won't sting you. Odd, but almost always true.

Years passed, without much garden activity, until the end of the war. After army adventures in places as far apart as the Western Desert, Greece, Abyssinia, South Africa and Burma, I found myself Comptroller of the Viceroy's Household in India. There we had a garden indeed, with gardeners innumerable. Harold Nicolson has described me in embarassingly glowing terms, in his introduction to one of my early books, as 'resplendent in a gold and white uniform presiding over the upkeep of the Lutyens gardens at Delhi, directing with a wave of his trowel that stupendous creation among the

Mr Luxmoore's garden, *opposite*, at Eton, where I learned the legend of the magic Brothers of the Rose, *above right*, and *left*: a show rose-garden with historic Syon House in the background.

cannas and the golden orioles: never since the days of Xenophon has a soldier . . . been so precise and efficient a gardener'. All very complimentary, fine and fancy, but I did achieve one major and useful alteration. I had a large area of the Viceregal Park dug up for growing vegetables, much needed in the several hospitals round New Delhi.

The man in charge of the Viceregal gardens was an imposing and immensely knowledgeable Englishman, Mr Reader: he was the archetype of an old-fashioned head gardener, always dressed in the heaviest tweeds on the hottest days; his only concession to its being India, and not Gloucestershire, the occasional straw hat.

Mr Reader had never had to deal with a Comptroller of the Household who took much interest in the gardens, and at first did not take me very seriously, but when he realised that I was really interested, we made good friends, and spent what were for me happy and instructive hours in the working area of the gardens, in the striped shadows of the 'chick' (slat) houses. He showed me how to take cuttings, make compost, prune such exotic plants as mandevilla (white lily flowers) and brunfelsia, the Flower of Yesterday (pale blue), Today (dark blue) and Tomorrow (white). Good training, but I fear not very useful when I returned to post-war England. But the seed had germinated, the cutting struck. The garden bug had bitten me.

Back in London, I wondered what I should do with my life. I found myself looking at gardens with a new eye, and even began to give advice, for which I did not charge, and which therefore was seldom followed. But from the happy day when I joined *House & Garden*, and started writing gardening articles, my knowledge, not only of plants, but of garden design grew apace. My taste developed and I inevitably gravitated to the gardening fraternity, picking up ideas and tips. From Vita Sackville-West, for instance, 'do not, as some grand gardeners do, despise the humble golden privet, and lobelia; not in rows, but spreading clumps can look very well; and golden privet, especially in London gardens, can light up the shadiest corner', and from Bobby James (after whom the rose is named) '*Il faut presenter un jardin*': why in French, I have no idea, but it means, I think, that when showing a garden, you should have a set itinerary, so that the visitor receives a series of pleasing and

At Holker Hall; *opposite*, Cark in Cartmel, Cumbria, Mr and Mrs Hugh Cavendish have had the originality to set out a formal parterre not with hybrid tea roses but with ornamental kale. *Above left*: the vast gardens of the Viceroy's house in India which were in my charge when Comptroller of the Household. *Above right*: The Vicomte Charles de Noailles, a great friend, and garden mentor.

contrasting impressions. I do not totally agree with that, but it does prevent you approaching a false perspective from the narrow end. Charles de Noailles, surely the only Frenchman ever to be a Vice-President of The Royal Horticultural Society, was an enchanting man, with perfect taste; it was he who told me never to plant Acer Negundo (white and pale green foliage) next to the red-leaved Prunus Pissardii, '*ça fait banlieu*'. It may 'make suburb', but the suburbs are full of attractive gardens. Charles also decreed that trellis-work must always be square – never diamond shaped. Such personal quirks and foibles are always worth listening to, and remembered, even if not meekly followed. Charles was full of them.

There were soon to be several important developments in my garden life. I began to be taken seriously as a designer. Russell Page became a helpful friend (more words of wisdom, eagerly stored up), and I commissioned the charming and gifted American, Lanning Roper, to write me an article for *House & Garden*. I think it was his first, on Day Lilies, of all rather dull subjects: perhaps that was why he took so long over it. Soon I was being asked to design gardens all over England and Scotland; also in America, in Florida and Long Island, with very different climates, but challenges: and many a great plus was that I made nice friends on the way.

But the most rewarding garden abroad, which I created, was in Provence. I am told, though I cannot remember it, that when first shown the untouched site, and asked if it had possibilities, I replied, 'Well, it will never be Versailles, but there are some nice trees'. And so there were; a rather neglected avenue of well-grown cypresses – a good start. As a lover of English gardens, I set about planning to include the three things which all Englishmen think essential in any garden – a lawn, a rose garden and a herbaceous border. Lawns are difficult in Provence, owing to lack of water, but it is nonsense to say that you need 100 years to make a good one. Thanks to a generous and enthusiastic patron, or rather, patronne, we converted the car parking area in front of the house into an excellent lawn in a year. Our rose garden could not be compared with the one at Syon, but we did not want that, we wanted roses that were good 'doers', like Iceberg which, in Provence, flowers from April till November, and Bobby James which scales 30-foot high trees, and, of course,

The enchanting and informal herbaceous border, *opposite* at Folkington Place also shown on pp74 . *Above*: The perfect English lawn at Compton Beauchamp near Wantage in Oxfordshire. We never achieved quite that perfection in Provence – see overleaf.

all summer, roses for cutting. For these we found using plants raised in France the best.

An herbaceous border – the third 'must' for me – was more difficult, and we never achieved a border even with the addition of shrub roses, like the one shown on page 14. But, by the use of coloured-leaved shrubs – silver, gold and pink, we conjured some very attractive corners. That old English favourite, Senecio Greyii did not like us, but Phlomis fruticosa which is almost exactly the same did, and provided essential glints of silver. Golden Euonymus lavished its largesse: red berberis flourished.

The Arabs used to say that water supplied the music of the garden, so we indulged in several fountains, one rather grand opposite.

This is a book of English gardens, and the garden I have just described in such detail, as a rule prover, is in France, but it embodies several garden features which are important to me, and will be continually demonstrated in the 30 or so English gardens which form the body of my book – Le Petit Fontanille has a garden which is near to my heart, and always will be.

I mentioned earlier in this introduction that several developments in my garden life happened at about the same time. I left out photography. Having had the luck to work with such prestigious garden photographers as Cecil Beaton and Anthony Denney, I can hardly claim to be an autodidact, and by keeping my eyes open, I learned a lot from them. All the photographs in this book are taken by me.

I have chosen to show about three dozen of my sort of gardens, and tried to point out why, to me, they are special. As far as possible, I have noted with appreciation the personal touches their owners have given them, sometimes so eye-catching as to set the mood for a whole garden, or one particular corner.

As a room should tell one something about its owner, so a garden should tell something of its creator, whether it is a garden of many acres, with ancestral cedars, fountains and time-worn statues: or whether it is a plot the size of a tennis court in outer London. After all, one often sees better grown roses in roadside gardens, than in the stateliest of statelies.

The larger fountain *opposite*, at Le Fontanille in Provence, which Ambassador Anne Cox Chambers added to her garden. The evening sun's rays glint on the water sprays and make the Triton's conch-shell glow. *Above*: On the terrace at Le Fontanille – a circular seat, and beyond, a lawn, replacing the old parking area. The cypresses we found already there.

Saling Hall

GREAT SALING, ESSEX

MR AND MRS HUGH JOHNSON

The fortunate visitor to Saling Hall, home of Mr and Mrs Hugh Johnson in Essex, feels, as soon as he enters the welcoming front door, that he is in the house of a couple who know what it is all about. As he drives up he sees not only fine trees, some 200 years old, but also some newly planted, the varieties carefully chosen as they would be by the writer of that prestigious work, *The International Book of Trees*. A few steps through a cool and elegantly arranged hall, takes him to a sunlit garden room – half greenhouse, half drawing-room, where refreshment in the form of a bottle of chilled white wine is ready on ice. Hugh Johnson has also written about wine, of course. The air is scented with tangy geraniums, and through the open door a burgeoning bush of Phlomis fruticosa peers in, as if wishing to join the party.

A sunfilled conservatory, *opposite*, with lolling hydrangeas, offers a warm sitting out place on the chilliest summer day. *Below*: herring-bone brick paths, lavender hedged, run between brimming flower borders.

Outside lies the old walled garden, as it has done since William III's day, complete with box hedges, brick paths set in a herring-bone pattern, and clipped Irish yews. The borders are planted with the best of old favourite English herbaceous plants, some surely dating from the days when Saling Hall was the home of that well-known gardener of half-a-century ago, Lady Carlisle.

Clumps of lilies are there together with the pungently scented Salvia turkestanica, a variety of the Elizabethan Clary; this is the plant of which Christopher Hussey once extolled the 'opalescent leaves'. In contrast are newer introductions, such as the Ligtu hybrids of alstroemeria (1838) and a flourishing specimen of that comparatively newly introduced tree (1950), the golden-leaved Robinia pseudoacacia Frisia, which Hugh Johnson himself has described as 'one of the most graceful and decorative of all garden trees'.

Not far away grows Sambucus plumosa aureus spreading its feathery foliage above pale pink sprays of spiraea. Nearby Miss Wilmott's Ghost, that old favourite among eryngiums, shows its spectral thistle heads. Ellen Willmott herself, living at not-far-away Warley, must surely have known the garden at Saling well. Nearby, in telling contrast to its dark background of evergreen, grows one of the best smaller trees of today, Cornus controversa, in its variegated form, making a brave show with its silver speckled branches.

So much for the old garden, happy in the shelter of its mellow walls. But there is another garden at Saling Hall, if twelve spreading acres, landscaped in the Brunonian manner, can be called a garden. Here, Hugh Johnson has done posterity a good turn, not only by making a lake, but by planting trees, chosen for their future form, which will take some years to reach maturity: an act of faith indeed. One of Saki's clever characters said that the comforting thing about trees is that they do not rush about, and ask one questions. The new trees at Saling are far too happily placed and comfortably planted to want to move. The only question is whether posterity will be as kind to them as the present. One can only hope so.

The bright flowers, *opposite*, of alstroemeria Ligtu with the ancient church tower of St James the Great. *Below*: A statue turns its back, refusing to pose. Beyond, the many windowed façade overlooks the garden.

A Phlomis fruticosa: *above*, peers into the sunlit interior of the conservatory. *Centre*: A spreading clump of tangy leaved Salvia turkestanica, raises spires of mauve flowers beneath the golden branches of pseudoacacia Frisia. *Right*: The smallest pond offers facilities for lush riparian planting of such damp loving subjects as ferns, hostas and the giant gunnera – a native of Brazil which tolerates the breezes of East Anglia.

Winslow Hall

BUCKINGHAMSHIRE

SIR EDWARD AND LADY TOMKINS

All the available evidence suggests that Winslow Hall was designed by Sir Christopher Wren. The records show that Wren's team of master craftsmen, who worked at St Paul's Cathedral and Hampton Court, also worked at Winslow. The gardens were laid out in 1695 by George London and Henry Wise, who were certainly employed by Sir Christopher on other occasions.

The 'Great Garden' lay north of the house and was planted with oak, elm and walnut, and bounded on either side by red brick walls. All that remains today are the red brick walls which now make the outside perimeter of the garden.

'When we bought the house in 1959', says Lady Tomkins, 'the garden had been neglected for many years. The grass was waist high, there were misshapen box trees on the lawn, and yew hedges had turned into trees, and there were relics of the war, such as concrete emplacements and piles of old car batteries.

'After we had cleared this up, we were left with a flat rectangle of grass, and beyond it, a horseshoe-shaped spinney with some fine trees that had been planted mainly at the turn of the century: elms (much older, of course), atlantica glauca cedars, limes, oaks, chestnuts, copper beech, acacia, and a short avenue of silver birch inter-planted with yew.

'Our problem was, what to do with this featureless rectangle of grass? We felt that we had to break up the straight lines by planting clumps of trees and shrubs in irregular bays on either side of the lawn. We wanted to

An inquisitive wisteria, *below,* has a look over a well tailored hedge at an enclosed garden decorated with imposing urns. *Opposite*: The façade of Winslow Hall, almost certainly designed by the great Sir Christopher Wren, overlooks a flight of stone steps, a pair of obelisks and a handsome old lead tank.

create the mystery of a garden, and at the same time to preserve the air of a park, which is the main feature of this garden. We relied for effect on contrasting foliage – blue, grey, silver, yellow, red, purple – and many variegated trees and shrubs, as well as light green, dark green and shiny evergreens, with blossom in spring and leaf-colour in autumn. We also looked for trees with striking bark, such as the acers Senkaki, Hersii, Forestii, griseum and pensylvanicum with its snakey bark, as well as several betulas, such as Jacquemontii, albosinensis, septentrionalis, and papyrifera. Other rewarding trees we found, were Eucalyptus niphophila, Prunus serrula, and Arbutus Unedo.

'A few really outstanding trees are Acer Cappadocium aureum, the American scarlet oaks, Quercus coccinea and rubra, Tulip Trees, and gingkos, which have such lovely, pale lemon-coloured leaves in autumn – the oldest known tree in the world.

'Shrub and bush roses grow well in the blue Oxford clay, as do the climbers, and our floribundas are establishing themselves well. Things that do particularly well are clematis, both the red and green smoke trees, Cotinus coggygria, are outstanding, an exochorda, most cotoneasters, and kolkwitzia, and of course, all the philadelphus.

'The garden is planted very much in the modern way, but we think it makes an attractive, and fairly labour-saving setting for the fine old house.'

No rose like Nevada, *above*, for long flowering and a galaxy of blossom. *Below*: A stone seat, with weeping pears Pyrus salicifolia, on either side,.with their mounds of silver foliage, in a setting of Crataegus Lavallei, ailanthus, and Acer Forrestii. *Opposite*: A free standing wisteria hangs a curtain of mauve flowers above the brighter colour of paeonies.

Sheepbridge Barn

EAST LEACH, GLOUCESTERSHIRE

SIR GUY AND LADY HOLLAND

White doves, *above*, were chosen rather than the more ordinary fantails. *Below right*: In the miniature courtyard the wall border is planted thickly with Arum italicum marmoratum with decorative marbled leaves in winter. *Left*: A colonnade of columns, eight out of eleven original Roman, leads to the front door.

Gloucestershire is a county of beautiful gardens, but how many can boast a colonnade of original Roman pillars? The seventeenth-century barn we show on these pages, with its subtly planted garden of greens and whites, is built on the site of one of the mutationes, which were built as staging-posts for the nearby Roman Akeman Street, which, 1,500 years ago, ran below the present house.

When the Hollands started to make the garden, in what was once the cattle yard, they found the whole area was floored with a two-foot layer of rammed stone. To make planting borders possible, deep trenches had to be excavated and filled with imported soil – local and full of lime. During the operation many pieces of Romano-British pottery were found.

The idea was for the garden to blend in with the green of the surrounding fields – in June, a cloudy forest of Cow Parsley. No bright colours, but only plants like John Evelyn's, A collection of 'Curious Greenes'. Too many greys would have looked too sophisticated – and in any case, most do not like the cold Cotswold winters.

Scotlands Farm

HENLEY, BERKSHIRE

MR MICHAEL AND THE HON MRS PAYNE

A brambly hollow offered the perfect site for the creation of a lake, thus fulfilling an ambition of the owners of this Berkshire garden. There have been many improvements and changes in the garden round Scotlands Farm in the last 50 years, but the greatest must surely be the creation of the lake. The Paynes, who moved in eight years ago, always wanted water somewhere in their garden. The lie of the land to the east of the house – an area overgrown with nettles and brambles, but a definite hollow – seemed to offer the ideal site for a stretch of ornamental water, set in a miniature eighteenth-century landscape, with large sweeps of grass and mature trees, including oaks, a giant weeping willow and two impressive taxodiums.

The house, *above*, was converted from an old chalk and flint barn. *Right*: Geraniums light up a shady corner. *Far right*: A brambly hollow offered the perfect site for the creation of a lake, thus fulfilling an ambition of the owners. Since this very successful first effort, they have conjured two more, smaller versions. The summer house was built after a design by Repton. In the foreground a clump of reeds assumes majestic proportions.

This important and picturesque addition to the garden was conjured five or six years ago, and now 'looks as if it has been there forever, with its large trees, golden orfe sunning themselves, mallard flying in and out, moorhens squawking and dragon-flies hovering. It has become a favourite part of the garden'. Recently two more lakes have been added, so Scotlands Farm has become even more attractive to water-loving wild life.

Planting round the lake has been given great thought, and though cornus, bergenia, gunnera and other classic water-side plants have been set in large clumps at the water's edge, the importance and pictorial value of spaces for reflection – and reflections – have not been forgotten.

Focal point of the whole scheme is the small rustic summer house. This was originally made for a recent Repton exhibition and was exhibited at the Victoria and Albert Museum in February 1983.

Two warnings to would-be lake makers: Heracleum giganteum can look 'stunning by the water' but is an appalling spreader and seedlings have to be ruthlessly weed-killed; and Elodea canadenis is often recommended by helpful friends to keep water aerated, but in the new lake at Scotlands Farm it has gone berserk, threatening to ruin the overall plan, and will have to be removed, a complicated operation.

There are many lessons to be learnt by visitors to this interesting garden. For example, the usefulness of some shrubs that many gardeners take for granted – white leaved Cornus alba elegantissima, for one, which shows up at a distance, has beautiful red stalks, providing a striking contrast with neighouring green-leaved shrubs, and is invaluable for flower arrangements all summer, and Eleagnus ebbingei which is often considered rather dull, but can be trusted to do well in almost any difficult place.

Sharp corners of flower borders at Scotlands Farm have been smoothed into curves, to make mowing easier; architectural features have been added, which are expensive to buy and install, but require little maintenance afterwards; new plantings have concentrated on plants of good and contrasting foliage, with scented plants set judiciously by seats and gateways. 'There are still many more things to be done . . . but that is all part of the fun, and is an everlasting and absorbing interest.'

Artemisia Palmeri, *above*, in a closely planted border stands out against dark foliage of a yew hedge. *Left*: An elegant stone sundial is set amid a carpet of Alchemilla mollis and lavender. *Opposite*: Pots and stone troughs brimming with annuals such as petunias and impatiens, on the sunfilled terrace.

Yarlington

NEAR WINCANTON, SOMERSET

THE COUNT AND COUNTESS DE SALIS

When Count and Countess de Salis first moved into their house near Wincanton, 23 years ago, there was virtually no garden. In the eighteenth century, a house of this type would certainly have had elegant walks through woody glades, and certainly a regimented rose garden. This last is, indeed, what they found, 'and immediately scrapped'.

Carolyn de Salis takes up the tale: 'My husband nor I barely knew the difference between a daffodil and a tulip, so for the first few years we had a happy time making mistakes. We planted out red salvias in rows which the mice fortunately ate, and willow trees in particularly dry corners.

'Then we took a grip of things and employed a landscape gardener. He suggested a fountain backed by herbaceous plants like delphiniums and lupins, but when my husband saw the plans his reaction was, "At last we know what we don't want".

'Six uninteresting trees were cut down and bonfires lit on the stumps, to make way for the area that is now the sunk garden. We built a three-sided wall, found some old paving stones from a church, and installed some statues brought from Italy. My husband made the plinths for them out of concrete.

'Having achieved this, we then set out the planting. A great friend of ours, Penelope Hobhouse, whose taste in garden design I have always admired, helped in the initial planning. We used olearias, escallonias and viburnums for evergreens, with clumps of variegated phormiums by the steps, to give something of a South of France look. The garden was then crammed with peonies, Regale lilies, herbaceous geraniums, phlox,

A statue, *opposite*, surveys the garden scene, set against a luxuriant bank of pale cool coloured flowers, special favourites at Yarlington. *Above*: A strong growing specimen of American Pillar which has doughtily and enduringly survived several doses of weedkiller, flowering profusely every year.

lavender, climbing roses, potentillas, masses of grey plants and cistus, and campanulas of all sorts. To give depth and lead the eye into the garden, we planted eight Phillyrea augustifolia, which I have since trained to look like puddings – very satisfactory. To balance this area we have planted a square of pleached limes – Tilia euchlora, the one that does not drop black messes – with rose beds and a lily pond in the middle. The roses are mostly rugosas: Frau Dagmar Hastrup, Blanc Double de Coubert, with Grass an Aachen, Little White Pet and The Fairy surrounding them. These beds we have underplanted with the non-flowering kind of grey Lambs Ears (Stachys lanata). The lily pond has proved the most difficult thing we have done. I never knew there was so much "life" in water and getting the water lilies going was a major achievement. But one day last summer I heard a visitor say "They are obviously great experts on water lilies". We now have an assortment floating happily around, but more by good luck than knowledge.

'I love pink and white flowers so both this area and the sunk garden tend to be with this colour scheme in mind. A little blue has crept in, but no yellow.

'On the south front of the house which is brick, we have planted various climbing roses – Golden Showers, Spek's Yellow and a banksia. We bought American Pillar with the house, and despite enormous doses of weedkiller she flowers profusely every year. It seems very mean to go on trying to annihilate her so, although she is not one of my favourites, I have given in. This area is very sheltered, so certain tender plants like variegated Pittosporum and Melianthus major do well here.

'The earth that came out of the swimming-pool has been used as a wind break. We have covered it with roses Bobby James, longicuspis and rubrifolia, an excellent ground cover if it can be kept within bounds.

'Our latest project is a great natural bowl in the woods. My husband cleared all the rough growth and we found that it was once terraced down to a pond at the bottom. There is even a tap. Presumably the Edwardians couldn't get it to hold water so gave up. Beside this there are some steps leading up to the remains of a Georgian summer house. One day we hope to rebuild it.

'Our beautiful walled kitchen garden has been neglected but we have more or less succeeded in ridding the soil of the dreaded bindweed and couch grass. It still has its original box hedges and, last summer, we had all sorts of delicious vegetables growing in lovely straight rows. I think a well-kept kitchen garden is a great delight.

Artemisia Palmeri, *opposite above*, with other silver leaved plants, used in many of the borders at Yarlington to set off bright colours and lighten dark corners, though most artemisias prefer full sun, as here. *Opposite below*: Water lilies were slow to establish themselves but now flourish. *Above*: Pots of white daisy trees, and time-weathered chairs outside the garden door.

'We have rebuilt the greenhouse and put a miniature extra-heated one inside for seed germination.

'My gardening begins in the spring as I don't like the cold. I go outside as little as possible in the winter months, apart from doing chores like pruning the roses. I love seeing the first snowdrops, and our drive yellow, with different daffodils. Every plant has its place. Hyde Park looks wonderful with massed tulips but I don't feel they would be right here. I use certain bedding plants like tobacco plants, pink and white petunias, and geraniums in tubs, which look good in a formal situation.

'Roses are such good value and do well with us. We can't grow azaleas and I couldn't be bothered to dig large holes and fill them with lime-free soil in order to try.

'A garden should be enjoyed and loved and not look too hoovered. With help from our only gardener, Mr Davis, we manage to keep ours moderately weed-free. I know one drive that looks as if it has been cut with nail scissors – far too manicured – but perhaps I am envious.'

The Grove

BRITWELL SALOME, OXFORDSHIRE

MR DAVID AND LADY PAMELA HICKS

David Hicks wanted an architectural garden with vistas and avenues of chestnut and *left*, hornbeam. The urn came from the Hicks' former garden at Britwell. *Above*: A porch in neat Chinese Chippendale-style. *Below*: A close-up of a garden fence, and wall piers crowned with five pinnacles.

For the house, which David Hicks has recently transformed, he decided that designing a new garden was a priority. 'Full of enthusiasm', he says, 'I started off by moving some old roses, as well as well-established rheums, hydrangeas and bergenias. Most of them to my surprise survived, some did not.

'Apart from a few old plants, all we found in the garden were good stone and brick walls, established trees, every sort of weed, broken china and a lot of oyster shells. The soil was poor and chalky, but we lavished dozens of bags of Arthur Bowers' compost on it, and our three horses produced for us ample presents of manure, which is laid down, sometimes for years, like port, before being used.

'I wanted an architectural garden, so I devised two main vistas to be seen from the drawing- and dining-rooms, composed of hornbeam and chestnut respectively, with a third, more natural, for the library.'

'Beside the walls, a few old farm buildings, including a coach-house and a dairy, divide the garden into ten separate areas. The front of the house looks east, out over a rough grass lawn of daffodils, narcissi and fritillaries, with a vast ilex beyond.

'The house is framed by brick walls into which I put Gothic-shaped doors. One leads into the south garden – all Regency striped lawn (50 per cent grass and 50 per cent moss) and a hornbeam palisade with matching hedges below. The hedges are L-shaped, with kickbacks at the two corners containing fine early eighteenth-century stone urns, which we brought from our old house, Britwell, nearby.

'I control the weeds under the trees with "Covershield" – most efficient. This vista is terminated by a dark-green, painted, wooden clairvoyée, on the original garden boundary wall, with brick piers surmounted with plywood pinnacles, which were inspired by ones at Derek Hill's house in Donegal.

'To the left, a tapestry tunnel surrounds a shrubbery, and leads to the right-hand compartment where I have planted two, long, wide herbaceous beds of crenellated plan. Each has a background of espaliered Albertine roses, and has four clumps of Phytolacca americana (in America its colloquial name is Virginia Poke), six clumps of saxifrage and three hydrangea "Madame Mouillière". I also planted masses of auratum and Regale lilies, Rosa viridiflora, Salvia turkestanica, Hosta Sieboldii for its wonderful blue-green leaves, pale-pink peonies, and different eremurus, with as many varieties of Mrs Sinkin and other scented dianthus as I can cram in, as ground cover.

'At the northern end, in a third bed, two open-work pyramids are smothered in honeysuckle, and Constance Spry stands on a carpet of Alchemilla mollis, walled in by artichokes and supported at the corners by yellow-flowered Peony lutea ludlowii. The middle is filled with "family roses", pale-yellow Mountbatten, Margaret von Hessen and Lady Romsey. Lord Louis, being deep, madder-red, has to be grown elsewhere, for the colour theme of this part of the garden is green of all

A gothic windowed façade, *opposite*, overlooks a flower bordered terrace. *Left above*: A crisp white obelisk rises from a bed of peonies, alchemilla and gypsophila. *Left*: A garden conceit, consisting of a rustic arch of South Sea shells, under-planted with Hosta Sieboldii, with its glaucous leaves. In the oval, a portrait in bronze relief, of Lady Mountbatten, Lady Pamela's mother.

sorts (particularly bindweed!), pale-pink, white, pale-mauve, with yellow accents.

'Passing through a Chinoiserie door is a long, narrow cutting-rose bed leading to Steve Madgen's cottage. Steve has cut our grass, planted trees, clipped our hedges and looked after the horses for 22 years. To the right, a door leads into the secret rose garden, all old species bushes and climbers, with a few honeysuckles, under-planted with chives, which are said to ward off black spot.

'I think that secret gardens should have only one terrace, so you turn round, and walk back round the farm buildings, past the swimming-pool, centred on the west facade of the house, and two L-shaped plantings on either side of Aesculus indica with matching edges. To the left of this compartment is the raised pot garden, where, I hasten to say, I do not smoke, but grow tulips, followed by geraniums, followed by bare soil for six months, in six low tubs.

'Then comes the old horse pond which I have resuscitated with generous clumps of Gunnera manicata, acanthus, Zantedeschia aethiopica (planted six inches below the water level, to protect them from frost), Heraculum giganteum, Peltiphyllum peltatum and Inula magnifica – all waterside plants, with imposing and contrasting leaves.

'It may sound didactic but I dislike valerian, variegated plants of any sort, versicolour roses, cotoneasters, asters or chrysanthemums. In my green-house I grow roses, geraniums, jasmine, daturas and clivias, but never strelitzia, African Violets, or bougainvillea, elegant though its name, and called after a great French sailor.

'What I have planted needs two men and lots of my time, but it has been planned in such a way that my son can "edit" whole areas without sacrificing anything from the house, and the tree planting will certainly be rewarding for my grandchildren.

'It is a garden for all season: my vistas of architectural trees look marvellous in the winter, as do the walls, hedges, and garden embellishments. My parents were both very keen gardeners, so it is hardly surprising that my garden gives me such great pleasure.'

A gate, *opposite*, between piers with canine finials. *Above right*: Old roses border a grass path leading to an arched entrance to a further garden. *Right*: A cloud of the flowers of Crambe cordifolia hovers over a dwarf standard of Nozomi roses. To the right, spires of eremurus make a picture full of incident.

Garsington Manor

OXFORDSHIRE

MR AND MRS L. INGRAMS

Garsington Manor, *left*, with its gabled windows, looking out over falling yew-hedged terraces of pigeon grey stone. On the lowest terrace a *pièce d'eau*, complete with recumbent water-god. *Right*: Low walls cushioned and curtained with the bright upholstery of spring. Much in evidence are white arabis and candy tuft, both old favourites in English gardens.

About sixty-three years ago, the church bells of the village of Garsington rang out a welcome to the new owners of the manor, Lady Ottoline and Philip Morrell. Little did the villagers know what fame the Morrells were going to bestow on the hitherto little-known name of Garsington. Lady Ottoline, a pacifist and certainly Bohemian, had a genius for friendship and was loved by many, and almost worshipped by a few. Her husband, Philip Morrell, was in a different key altogether, unpopular in politics, a radical pacifist, but a devoted husband and perfect foil to his effulgent wife.

They were to make Garsington a famous centre of entertainment. Lady Ottoline, in her memoirs, describes their way of life. Sometimes, she felt as if their much-loved house and garden were a theatre where 'week after week a travelling company would arrive and play their parts'. The old grey Jacobean house stood 'like a casket', hung with roses. And of the garden, for these notes are about the garden rather than the house, she wrote, '. . . the forecourt enclosed by stone gates and dark walls of yew', the formal garden 'like a coloured sweet smelling carpet . . . below the terraces, monastic fish ponds . . . with cypresses, Italian statues, romantically crumbling, with a background of dark cobweb-hung yew, and grass paths where, in those days, peacocks spread their tails, or unfolded them with amorous vibrations'. Lady Ottoline loved and remembered everything: the roosting peacocks with their long iridescent hanging tails, the moonlight on the courtyard 'still and silent, as if spellbound, making the white flowers whiter'. In spring, she would lean out of her window, to touch and smell the pink blossoms of an old pear tree.

The garden certainly made a perfect theatre, where week after week a new company would arrive, shake out their frills and improvise a new scene in life. 'Philip and I raised the curtain, fate prompted the players'.

And what players they were: Aldous Huxley, Lytton Strachey, 'Carrington' and Katherine Mansfield, who thought of making the garden at Garsington the scene

in a book, with people walking in pairs deep in conversation, glancing at one another as they passed, '. . . a kind of musical speaking conversation set to flowers'. The flowers of the garden at Garsington, half-a-century ago, were zinnias, sunflowers, snap-dragons, all tinted a little too vibrantly perhaps, for today's taste; but perfect as a setting for Lady Ottoline's favourite Russian Ballet colouring.

The guests were varied. Charlie Chaplin, D. H. Lawrence and the then Prime Minister, Mr Asquith. Once, when he unexpectedly approached the pool, one of the house-maids, who was taking a surreptitious dip, pretended to drown 'to attract attention', and was saved by Oscar Wilde's friend, Robbie Ross, who jumped into the water in his best suit, having prudently removed his watch.

The Morrells left their much-loved home in the 'twenties, because, it was said, Lady Ottoline was so upset by the news that a large branch of a favourite ilex had broken off.

The cast at Garsington changed, but only up to a point. I first heard of it when I was quite young, dining with the then Lord Gerald Wellesley, an architect, and Edward Knoblock, who is said to have invented the fashion for Regency furniture. Both criticised the house as 'not their period', but remembered how it smelled deliciously of Auratum lilies, and, Gerry added, slightly unkindly I thought, of mice.

When I first went there my hostess was Lady Wheeler Bennett who, as I remember, had also just entertained the Prime Minister at luncheon, and was expecting his predecessor in office to tea. Garsington life went on.

The house is very fortunate in its present owners, Mr and Mrs Ingrams. When I rang up and asked if I could come, and add to my already large collection of Garsington pictures, I was asked to postpone my visit until the new spring planting of tulips was in flower.

It is heart-warming to see this beautiful garden, so full of echoes of life as it was lived, even in the twenties, in very few English country houses, as well cared for as it is today. The parterre, with its panels of brilliant colour, is as eye-catching every spring as it was half-a-century ago. The roses smell as sweetly. Mr and Mrs Ingrams are to be congratulated on their taste.

I am grateful for information gained from the late Robert Gathorne-Hardy's excellent version of Lady Ottoline Morrell's memoirs.

Overlooking the great parterre, *opposite*, is a seventeeth-century dove-house. The box edged flower beds have been symmetrically planned and recently generously replanted by Mr and Mrs Ingrams. Slim clipped yews give the garden an air of Italy. *Below left*: Twin conifers invite the visitor to a flight of low stone steps. To the left, a cascade of cherry blossom makes a wall of flowers. *Below right*: The rustic architecture of the steps and terrace outside the east door of the manor was devised by Lady Ottoline Morrell's husband.

Burford House

TENBURY WELLS, WORCESTERSHIRE

MR JOHN TREASURE

When the gardens were completely redesigned by John Treasure in 1954, he had in mind that one day they would be open to the public, so that plants, trees and shrubs could be seen and enjoyed in surroundings other than those of a nurseryman's nursery.

The gardens, and nursery which adjoins them, attract visitors from many parts of the country, and from Europe, USA, Australasia and the Far East. During the last ten years visitors have had the opportunity of seeing trees and shrubs reaching maturity, as it is now 27 years since the first were planted.

John Treasure has, in recent years, been able to use the skill of plant association to the full. The association of foliage, form, flowers and fruit gives the imaginative visitor endless ideas that they can use for planting schemes in their own gardens. A speciality of the gardens is the number of different kinds of clematis which are grown. Most of the plants grown in the garden are offered for sale in the nursery. Visiting the gardens and nursery is of the greatest interest for plantsmen, and full of ideas for flower arrangers too.

Formal greenery, *opposite*, where a telling feature is a symmetrical planting of conifers round a central pool, with plantings of red dwarf dahlias beneath. *Top left*: In the courtyard there is a pool surrounded by lush foliage plants, and cheered by the pink flowers of hydrangea. To the left, a bold plant of Juniper sabina tamariscifolia. *Top right*: The golden foliage of Chamaecyparis obtusa Crippsii contrasting with the giant leaves of Gunnera manicata. *Above left*: Close planting of Anemone japonica and pink schizostylis suppress weeds. *Above right*: Rich colour supplied by Crocosmia Emberglow and Cotinus Royal Purple. Beyond, the golden leaves of Catalpa bignonioides.

Parkside

WINDSOR GREAT PARK

THE EARL AND COUNTESS OF DROGHEDA

The late Georgian façade, *left*, of Parkside House with its glistening white walls and large windows. The garden is sheltered by a protective belt of mature trees. *Below left*: An elegant Victorian Scissor Back seat, set in front of a sunny wall and embowered in roses. *Below right*: A thickly planted rose border shown here in full flower, effectively edged with low growing silver-leaved plants and defined by stone paving.

Parkside, the country home of Lord and Lady Drogheda, lies next door to the Savill Gardens. The house itself was built about 1800 and subsequently enlarged, but it retains its late-Georgian walls and large windows giving on to a flower-filled garden.

Lord Drogheda does not think highly of the soil in his garden though it seems to offer sustenance to a variety of plants of different tastes. Rhododendrons and azaleas proliferate in the surrounding woodland, and are bright with colour in spring, glowing in the half-shade provided by a scarlet oak, an immense ilex and an impressive lime. White daffodils are planted in wide groups near the front lawn and several different kinds of magnolias, all planted in the last 25 years, open their sweetly scented flowers every spring.

But, it is in June and July that the garden at Parkside is really at its peak, the air heavy with the breath of roses and the tang of philadelphus. A graceful arch-shaded path leads from the garden door of the house down to the lily pond, and is a most attractive feature. The arches are festooned with vines, clematis

(which respond gratefully to feeding) and one of the best of all Bourbon roses, Kathleen Harrop, with its delicate shell-pink recurrent flowers.

The lily pond, with a child in lead clasping a fish, is planted round not only with moisture-loving plants but with prostrate junipers,, with their blue-green, weed-smothering foliage.

The large, sunk rose garden is another important area of the garden at Parkside. Here is to be found that star among shrub roses – Raubritter. Other favourites are Albertine and François Juranville, two roses with pretty pink flowers described by the great Vita Sackville-West as looking as if they had 'fallen into a tea-cup'. Two roses with similar-sounding names also find a place: the musk rose Felicia, cut down every year to make a shapely bush, and Felicité et Perpétue, a sempervirens hybrid which loves to climb through the branches of a tree. There is a fable worth recounting about this two-named rose: Felicité and Perpétue were two young Christian virgins who suffered martyrdom

Foxgloves stand tall, *opposite*, at the entrance of a pergola-shaded path with a classical bust glimpsed at the end of the vista. Vines and clematis festoon the arches. *Below*: A stone vase brimming with long flowering fuchsias, stands in a sheltered corner of the walled garden. Beyond, a stretch of impeccably mown lawn.

together in Carthage for their faith. It is said that St Perpétue had a vision of a flowering ladder leading upward to heaven, just as the rose named after her mounts through branches towards the sky in our gardens today.

Many other roses are famous for the show they make when planted to climb up trees rather than against a wall: Emily Grey, Commandant Beaurepaire and Wedding Day to name but three. The theory is that the air blowing freely through their leaves keeps them happy, and prevents the mildew they might suffer if confined against a wall.

Before leaving Lord and Lady Drogheda's garden, one clever gardening device must be noted. Among the roses in the rose garden are planted other plants which, at a distance, give the appearance of being roses, and so, when the first flush of hybrid teas, in particular, is over, some show of colour is maintained. In the garden at Parkside, that splendid plant Lavatera olbia rosea is used in this way.

The lily pond, *left*, has a child in lead clasping a fish. *Below*: Long flowering Lavatera olbia planted among rose bushes, makes a brave show long after the roses are past their best – an excellent gardening tip.

The Old Rectory

BURGHFIELD COMMON

MR AND MRS RALPH MERTON

Ralph and Esther Merton came to Burghfield in early spring 1950. That May, to please her mother-in-law, Mrs Merton went, for the first time, to the Chelsea Flower Show. In her own words, 'My mother-in-law was a quicksilver lady, who shot up and down aisles – with me lumbering behind. But I bought six clematis – from Pennells – and was hooked on gardening from then on.'

'In those days', Mrs Merton goes on, 'the garden had lots of fiddly rose beds, long since scrapped, and not a single camellia or magnolia. I imagined that the soil must be unsuitable for such treasures, but not a bit of it. We discovered that we were on dead neutral clay, and could grow almost anything if we took trouble. So I started to plant all kinds of roses – "old-fashioned" and climbers in particular – and I learned to underplant them with romantic, sweet-smelling, cool-coloured things, which look beautiful, and smother weeds, too. I avoided bright colours, though some have crept in here and there.

'I wanted to be able to pick something every day, but when plants begin to flower in mass and look beautiful I cannot bear to cut them, so I made a cutting-garden in the kitchen garden. In the past few years, I have been lucky to have been aided and abetted in all these activities by our wonderful gardener, Trevor Last.

'I grow Helleborus torquatus, not only for my pleasure, but to impress gardeners, and sweet peas for lesser mortals. I also grow nettles for butterflies, and ground elder because I can't get rid of it.

'The statue in the pond is Roman, and came from Wilton. It used to stand in the middle of a duck-weed lawn – which, in its way, was rather pretty – but my husband was clever enough to find a product called Clarosan from Ciba Geigy which cleared the weed and did not harm the plants round about.

The summer house, *opposite*, which Esther Merton describes as designed by her husband with some help from Claud Phillimore. *Above:* The older part of the house faces down a broad grass path between herbaceous borders. The yellow flowers are long flowering Lysimachia punctata.

A Roman statue, *right*, in a watery setting. To the *left*, pink flowered Spiraea filipendula rubra. *Left:* Low cushions and mats of brightly coloured alpines are encouraged to encroach on the softly coloured gravel in pleasing contrast. *Below:* A garden seat fairly embowered in the flowers and leaves of Geranium maderiensis. *Above:* Burghfield Old Rectory presents a perfectly proportioned Georgian façade.

Thompson's Hill

SHERSTON, WILTSHIRE

MR AND MRS SEAN COOPER

When Sean and Evelyn Cooper found their present house, Thompson's Hill, on the outskirts of the beautiful old village of Sherston in Wiltshire, about four years ago, it was a 'totally dilapidated' ancient cottage. It stood in half-an-acre of ground, part of which was being used as a transport yard, with sheds, buildings and concrete, all enclosed with half-ruined walls. What free ground there was, was overgrown with nettles and brambles, elders and the wrecks of a few old trees. Any of these worth keeping and making use of were, of course, kept: among them a big yew tree, two apples and two cherries.

Evelyn Cooper is a perceptive and experienced gardener. The site of the future garden had good views towards a green hillside with a tiny river flowing at its base. On the other side lies the village of Sherston, 'lovely old roofs by day, and sparkling house lights by night'.

An energetic farmer friend with an excavator soon cleared the area of the garden-to-be. Mrs Cooper then went over the levelled ground with Tumbleweed to clear it of weeds. After a surprisingly short time she was able to sow grass, and once it was established, she laid out her garden.

Using some long ropes, the Coopers marked out where the beds were to go. In September, three years ago, they started to plant. Sean Cooper – an expert amateur carpenter – heightened some of the walls with trellis; these are now covered with roses, golden hop and clematis.

The Coopers' aim was to have a formal area near the house, and a stone terrace. The six-sided garden room, now in place, was built by Sean Cooper himself. It is 'endlessly sunny', and constantly in use.

The aim has been to plant for contrast in foliage as well as flower, a lavish use of ever-golds, ever-silvers and ever-greens important when the whole garden is within view of the house all the year round. The happy result is constant colour.

Most shrubs and roses thrive at Thompson's Hill, the climbing rose Madame Gregoire Staechelin is sensational. On some walls grow vines with edible fruit.

One looming problem: 'We planted everything too close together, so secateurs are constantly in use'.

The garden at Thompson's Hill, *opposite*, where the borders are closely planted to smother weeds as well as for showing season-long colour. The few old trees were carefully preserved. *Above left*: Of all wall growing roses Madame Grégoire Staechelin must surely take the prize. Only sadness – she only flowers once. *Right*: Viburnum Mariesii with its oriental tiers of flowered branches is an ideal plant for a medium-sized garden.

In the foreground, *left*, a bold group of iris, Kelways Canary Bird. Beyond the sexagonal garden house built by Sean Cooper himself. *Above*: A Goat's Rue worth looking for; flowering in a rich shade of blue, and growing in a pleasingly compact habit, this unnamed galega was a present from a gardening friend to Evelyn Cooper – identification unknown. *Below*: Golden privet is a much underrated plant and the great gardener Vita Sackville-West valued its bright colour, using it extensively at Sissinghurst. At its feet, a carpet of that excellent groundcoverer, Geranium sanguineum lancastriense.

The Physic Garden

CHELSEA EMBANKMENT

The Chelsea Physic Garden was founded in 1673 by the Society of Apothecaries. Its object, then, as it is today, was to cultivate, examine and learn more about plants. The Physic Garden has done important work through three centuries, though its career has had its ups and downs. That it has survived, according to the learned Professor W. T. Stearn, is because, at every crisis in the garden's long history, 'there were men conscious enough of its worth or potentialities, or proud enough of its past services to ensure its maintenance'.

The site chosen by the Apothecaries was suitable for several reasons. On the banks of the then clean, gleaming Thames, the area was not only salubrious, but easy to get to in those sensible days when the river was used as an artery for speedy and pleasant travel.

At first, things were difficult, but in 1676 funds were raised to build a wall round the newly laid-out garden to protect it from wind and robbers. Soon after, the prestige of the Physic Garden was such that there were interchanges of plants, which have continued ever since, between Chelsea and the great Botanic Gardens of the Continent, such as Leiden and Paris.

But a 'down' came in the garden's story when John Watts, who was appointed curator in 1680, got into such debt that the society had to get rid of him and 'came near to getting rid of the garden as well'. The situation was only saved by the appointment in 1693 of one Samuel Doody (1656-1706), an apothecary of 'uncommon sagacity' who retrieved the situation.

A young medical student from Ireland, Hans Sloane, had visited the garden in 1684. Sloane, in later years, was to play a very important part in the garden's story.

The young Irishman was impressed, as was John Evelyn, by the heated greenhouses and the methods employed by Watts of nursing tender plants through the English winter. Years after, in 1719, when running expenses were once more becoming a serious worry, Sloane, no longer poor and obscure, had become a Chelsea landowner and President of the Royal College

A statue of Sir Hans Sloane (1660-1753), *opposite*, a great benefactor to the Physic Garden; Sloane Street in London is named after him. *Above*: Looking towards the laboratory and curator's house; in the foreground the misty blue flowers of Ceratostigma Willmottianum, named after the great Edwardian amateur gardener, Miss Ellen Willmott.

of Physicians. He was rich enough to buy the Manor of Chelsea, including the Physic Garden itself. From then on, for many years, the garden prospered.

Sloane had been made a baronet in 1716 and, in a document dated 20th February 1722, expressed his intention 'that the said Garden may at all times hereafter be continued as a Physic Garden and for the better encouraging the said Society to support the charge thereof for the manifestation of the power, wisdom and glory of god in the works of the creation, and that their apprentices and others may the better distinguish good and useful Plants from those that bear resemblance to them, and yet are hurtful, and other the like good purposes'. Which as Professor Stearn points out, 'shrewdly unites the pious and the practical'.

The distinguished Philip Miller, author of the prestigious *Gardeners' Dictionary*, became, certainly on Sloane's recommendations, curator in 1722, and remained at the Physic Garden till 1770. Under his direction the garden achieved international renown and was visited by all the great gardeners of the day.

However, in the last century there came a serious drop in the garden's fortunes and more financial crises. Staff was reduced, the greenhouse demolished, and all the important heating cut off. In 1893 things were at their very worst and a notice was put up announcing that the garden was to be sold for development. However, once more the axe was stayed. The Charity Commissioners were persuaded to accept a scheme by which the garden was to be in the joint care of various worthy bodies working together under the London Park Charities; thus the Apothecaries were relieved of the financial burden they had borne for so long.

From 1899 to 1937, William Hales, born in 1874, was curator, administering the garden with great skill. Under his direction the garden took on the brilliant appearance that it has today. As a working botanic garden, however, Chelsea's role is not primarily to be ornamental, but to facilitate botanic research, which is actively pursued to this day. For this reason, therefore, while always available to teachers and their students concerned in the study of botany, it is not generally open to members of the public. Fellows of the Royal Horticultural Society may apply to the Society for tickets for the occasional Open Days, announced in its journal.

The Physic Garden, older by nearly 200 years than Kew, is an oasis of green in the heart of London, of great botanical as well as historical interest, and should, at all costs be preserved.

A pool, *opposite*, with many plants of different forms growing happily with their feet in water: among them that British aquatic, Typha latifolia or reed mace, and the flowering water hyacinth – Eichornia speciosa, a rampant spreader. *Above*: A 'family' bed, containing different types of hemlock.

Winfield House

REGENT'S PARK

H.E. THE AMERICAN AMBASSADOR

In spring daffodils and narcissus grow happily beneath Lord Hertford's trees, *opposite*. *Above*: The classical façade of Winfield House overlooks a spreading lawn, the second biggest in London.
Below right: One of a pair of eagles given to the garden by Ambassador and Mrs David Bruce.

During the developments of Regent's Park in the early years of the last century, one of the most elegant houses was designed by Decimus Burton for the Marquess of Hertford, the model, it is said, for Lord Steyne in Thackeray's *Vanity Fair*. Lord Hertford certainly had a shaky reputation, but his taste for beautiful ladies and beautiful houses was never in question. In a book, *Metropolitan Improvements*, published in 1827, his new 'suburban retreat' was described as not only elegant, but with 'buildings and offices ... in accordance with the wealth of their noble owner'. There was no mention of the garden, though we can be sure that some of the fine old trees which surround and, sadly, today, only partially conceal encroaching London, were part of Lord Hertford's original planting. The twelve-acre garden must surely be the second largest, after that at Buckingham Palace, in London. But, from the terrace of the present building, some

By the door, *above*, on to the terrace geraniums and the soaring leaves of dracaena fill a stone vase. *Below left*: A seat between luxurious clumps of shrubs catches all the sun. *Below right*: In summer the formal silver beds are replanted with pink geraniums. *Opposite*: Crisp white painted trellis, twelve year old box hedges and cobbled paths set in brick provide a harmonious decor.

signs of the outside world are evident. The top of the Post Office Tower, and the dome of the mosque do peer over the encircling trees.

As to the present building, the Hertford family sold their 'suburban retreat' after a fairly short tenure, and the house ended up as St Dunstan's Home for the Blind. Finally, in the 'thirties, it was bought by Barbara Hutton, who pulled it down, and built the present handsome red brick edifice. One regrets it was not in stucco, like the other Regent's Park houses and terraces, but it is a worthy building, and 50 London winters have mellowed it. Used as an American Officers' Club in the war, the house was eventually presented in 1946 by Barbara Hutton, with great generosity, to the United States, as their Ambassador's residence in London. It has been happy in its successive occupants, but seldom so happy as today.

Outgoing American Ambassadors have given generous legacies to Winfield House. Great improvements to the greenhouses and garden were made during the legendary era of David and Evangeline Bruce.

Walter and Lee Annenberg made princely donations towards the embellishment of the house itself – just two examples being the papering of one of the largest reception rooms with an historic Chinese wallpaper, and the addition to the entrance hall of a suite of eighteenth-century furniture worthy of the Victoria and Albert Museum.

The beautiful rose garden, designed by Sir Peter Shepheard and laid out by the prestigious Clifton Gardens, was donated in 1983 by John and Jo Louis and the Lila Acheson Wallace Foundation.

About sixteen years ago I was asked by the Annenbergs to help design the box garden outside the dining-room, now looking splendidly mature, and also the trellis-work on the walls.

Recently, it was a great joy to be called in to make some last-minute changes to the immediate surroundings of the house, to celebrate the visit of the President of the United States and Mrs Reagan. The present Ambassadorial pair, Charles and Carol Price, were an inspiration with their encouragement and enthusiasm. They conjured some beautiful new terrace furniture from America, and I found some elegant – and practical – garden chairs made of aluminium in Chinese Chippendale style from Lavender Hill. I widened a flower border outside the yellow drawing-room, always filled, as are all the rooms of Winfield House, with Carol Price's very special choice of flowers. This border I planted with long-flowering shrubs and plants. On either side of the terrace, I created two formal beds of silver Cineraria maritima and pink geraniums, interspersed with miniature conifers. One spring, mauve tulips preceded the geraniums, a happy combination with the silver.

To the terrace itself, we added some spectacular stone vases, and filled them not only with geraniums, but also with dracaenas; their soaring leaves would provide an almost pyrotechnic welcome.

The President and Mrs Reagan, for security reasons, were due to arrive by helicopter, not at the front door, but on the garden side. There was a moment of anxiety about whether some of my new plantings would be blown away. Especially vulnerable were six new conical bay trees from Belgium, and I had placed them, I thought, in the right spot, on the terrace, but where they would have to stand up to the full blast of the helicopter's landing. However, I was told that there were going to be security men behind every tree, and the ones stationed, in white gloves, behind the new bays, had the additional duty imposed on them, of holding them up; and all was well.

Airy metal structures, *opposite*, promise support for climbing roses in the rose garden which was a present to Winfield by Ambassador and Mrs John Louis. *Below left*: Thickly flowering roses border a trimly laid stone path. *Above*: A cupola shaped framework outlined against the sky. *Below right*: A balustraded terrace complete with comfortable white metal chairs and white umbrella can be seen beyond the white coigns and red brick of the house itself.

Folkington Place

POLEGATE, SUSSEX

COMMANDER AND MRS HENDRIK VOORSPUY

The picture *opposite* was taken by the author, of a group of mixed pots of flowers on the steps of a little used garden door of Folkington Place. It so struck the eye of a promising young painter of Atlanta, Georgia – Ronald Crawford, that he based a picture on it, now in the author's possession; it was the first of several paintings based on Peter Coats' photographs which have been exhibited successfully. *Above*: A group of papery petalled Romneya coulteri – the Californian Poppy. *Right*: The house from the flower filled garden, with orange red-hot pokers (kniphofia) showing their burning 'pokers' against a dark background of yews.

Some years ago I was taken by a friend to see a neighbour's garden: 'It is very pretty', she told me. I have often been promised very pretty gardens, and quite often found them – Dorothy Perkins roses and all. But Mrs Hendrik Voorspuy's garden at Folkington Place was a revelation, and one of the most exciting gardens I saw that year. Not only was it full of ideas – just one being the accent on plants which actually die decoratively – but all the colours themselves seemed subtly different to those in other gardens . . . pinks, silvers, dusty browns, pearly mauves. The chalky, stony earth of the East Sussex Downs was completely carpeted and cushioned with flowers, and the flint walls were curtained with roses, clematis and vines. Here was gardening at its most sophisticated, and although the overall effect was one of simplicity, I quickly recognised how much thought, plant knowledge and artistic eye had been needed to achieve the final effect.

I was told that when Commander and Mrs Voorspuy came to Folkington in 1959, all they found was a hay field with one overgrown herbaceous border facing

north, and one small lawn. All the rest was vegetable garden. But they were lucky to inherit, as well, a few Irish yews, one or two old apples, and some good old cobble and brick paths.

One of the Voorspuys' cares was to make a terrace of old York paving in the sheltered well of the house. The whole of the vegetable garden they grassed over, leaving a few old apple trees. In this ready-made, but at first flowerless frame, the garden grew up year by year. Mrs Voorspuy gives full credit for the garden's present beauty to a friend, Miss Priscilla Coventry, a pensioner who lived in the cottage. 'Miss Coventry was the genius behind the scenes', says Mrs Voorspuy. 'I am only under-gardener and odd-job man. Miss Coventry was trained at Studley and literally painted with flowers'. How successful Miss Coventry's 'pictures' are can be seen, I hope, from our photographs, though the garden at Folkington needs 20 pages in colour to do it justice.

Mrs Voorspuy concentrates – and I think that is what gives the garden its natural look – on species and many native wild flowers. For instance, a rare blue form of Scarlet Pimpernel is allowed to seed, as are Milk Thistles, white Marsh Mallows, Sweet Cicely, angelica, and many different herbs. There are very few modern plants – only some carefully chosen dahlias and a few tulips. Most of the roses are 'old' ones.

I asked Mrs Voorspuy about her 'decorative diers' and she gave me a list of her favourites, many of which she uses for drying as winter decoration. These included eupatorium, teazle, Cardoon, leeks, Pampas grasses, Allium albo pilosum, and various 'everlasting' flowers such as helichrysum and xeranthemum. One of the most spectacular, when I was first at Folkington, was a nigella with shiny red and green whiskered seedpods.

Grey plants are Mrs Voorspuy's special love, and they grow particularly well for her. Two she mentioned with pride were an Artemisia arborescens which has grown six feet high, and survived several winters on the south wall, and a special Lavendula stoechas from Spain with strongly scented foliage. Not only flora but fauna, too, seem happy at Folkington. In those days the whole Voorspuy family adored animals, and kept horses. The children had various pets, and were fond of reptiles, particularly snakes. Last year they had a badger that came every night for his supper, and all the robins and blue tits in the garden are hand-tame.

One of the rules of the garden at Folkington is 'no poisonous sprays whatever', and Mrs Voorspuy relies on feeding the plants well to combat disease. Occasionally the garden suffers from spraying from neighbouring farms and one magnificent horse chestnut of vast age and in full flower, was killed by sprays 'bouncing across the Downs'. Mrs Voorspuy found it with all its candles upside down.

Perhaps that is why, when I asked what her ideal of a garden was, she replied nostalgically: 'A peaceful one, full of birds and butterflies, sheltered from the prevailing wind . . . with beautiful plants arranged in as happy associations of colour and foliage as possible'.

Poppies, *below left*, and a dozen mixed flowers make a rich border. *Below right*: A gate in an old flint wall leads to the important working area of the garden. *Opposite*: A glimpse of the house between tall evergreens, with a magnificent herbaceous border, with its effulgent colours, in the foreground.

Cornwell Manor

KINGHAM, OXFORDSHIRE

THE HON PETER AND MRS WARD

The garden of Cornwell Manor is happy in many ways. Happy in its verdant Oxfordshire setting, with its never failing natural water supply, and happiest of all in the taste and affection lavished on it by its owners – and its devoted head gardener, Mr Hatchett.

When Peter Ward acquired Cornwell Manor some 25 years ago, the thoughtful landscaping of previous owners had grown to maturity. A nearby stream had been gently harnessed into a series of canals through the garden itself, bringing sparkle to a rock garden and permanent refreshment to a bog garden, before emptying its water into a series of small lakes. The terraces were already there, their balustrades clothed with clematis and roses, and linked with flights of shallow, comfortable steps.

In spring, the outlying areas of the garden are bright with daffodils. The garden, David Hatchett admits, was – and still is – labour intensive, but the original labour force of about a dozen gardeners is now down to three. He adds philosophically, 'But we cope'.

The garden and its surroundings are studded with interesting trees such as Acer griseum, with its peeling bark revealing under-bark of shining mahogany, and colouring brilliantly in autumn. Nearby grows Magnolia obovata, with its purple buds (always a point of interest on 'open days'), the sweet-smelling Osmanthus delavayi, and the long flowering Hamamelis mollis pallida with cool lemon-tinted flowers.

With a pool, *opposite*: in the foreground, Cornwell Manor
lies in as beautiful a garden as any in Oxfordshire.
Above: A statue on a graceful 18th century plinth, in a
setting of greenery, and pink and white peonies.

When I visited the garden, it was in high summer, and it was full of flowers, such as the white hardy agapanthus, as well as the transcendent Alstroemeria Ligtu hybrids, in their dozen warm shades, perfect flowers for cutting. Peony mlokosewitchii, colloquially Molly the Witch, had shed its pale yellow petals, but its decorative pods are almost equally eye-catching when they split open to show their scarlet and black seeds. These are just three notable plants, each of the highest quality.

The soil of the garden at Cornwell Manor is variable, 'lime bordering to neutral, over-lying oolite, and almost unworkable in winter'. All lime-loving plants such as viburnum, dianthus and campanulas do well, as do most plants of Chinese origin.

David Hatchett has a very definite garden philosophy. He considers that a garden must retain a feeling of tranquillity and peace, and the very essence of a country garden. He dislikes most modern insecticides and weedkillers and only uses them as a last resort. He feels that garden science is progressing – if it is progressing – too fast, at the expense of commonsense and true understanding of plants. Many of the old-fashioned remedies he thinks are still the best. 'I would like to see',

A sheltered corner, *opposite*. A paved terrace lies below the walls of the house, caparisoned with blue nepeta and furnished with well planted tubs and an inviting seat in the Chinese Chippendale taste. *Above*: An unusual pot-plant, a Kalmia latifolia, flourishes in specially prepared acid soil, in a capacious tub – a brilliant idea for gardeners in a relentlessly alkaline locality. *Below*: No better shrub for a warm sunny situation than Phlomis fruticosa with its leaves of grey velvet and luxurious habit.

he says, 'some of the so-called experts working here on a cold winter's morning, in a Cotswold frost and a howling wind blowing through the valley.

David Hatchett can certainly turn a phrase, as is to be expected of someone who published a successful book in 1983, *Country House Garden* (David & Charles), which describes a typical working year as head gardener at Cornwell Manor.

This is one of the most rewarding gardens in Oxfordshire to visit, as a 1,000 people did, recently, one fine spring day.

Beyond a cooling fountain, *left*, flights of shallower steps lead upwards between curtains of greenery. *Above left*: Walls of sun faded brick offers shelter for a galaxy of flowers, making a perfect background.
Right: Silver-leaved weeping pears (Pyrus salicifolia) line an imposing canal. *Below*: One of the best of all recently introduced trees – golden leaved Frisia pseudo-acacia.
Beyond, an 18th century dovecote.

Kingsmead

DIDMARTON, GLOUCESTERSHIRE

THE EARL AND COUNTESS OF WESTMORLAND

At the end of the main axis of the garden, *left*, a new gate, incorporating the initial of the owner, set between ball capped pillars and almost smothered in Rambling Rector roses. *Top*: A brimming flower box on a terrace corner, with white painted furniture. *Above*: A neatly proportioned gazebo, with a conical roof.

Of their garden at Didmarton in Gloucestershire, Lady Westmorland writes: 'When we moved into our house 14 years ago, there was a very nice garden but not exactly what we wanted. It consisted of a lawn with rose beds, an herbaceous border and a rather too large kitchen garden.

'But there were pros as well as cons. The kitchen garden was surrounded by a 10-foot high wall, a golden asset despite the fact that quite a large section of it blew down, soon afterwards, in a freak storm. It was quite soon repaired by the kind insurance people, leaving a promising dip in the middle, revealing a beautiful view over the greenest of pastures. Gales do not appear to be acts of God in Gloucestershire.

'To begin with (when our children were small) the "potager" was enclosed, within the surrounding wall, by a robust Chinese Chippendale fence. Robust because it had to be pony-proof. The space between the fence and the surrounding wall became a mown walk, with the elegant fence – complete with ponies' faces peering over it – on one side, and a mass of roses, clematis and other climbers covering the wall on the other.

'Some years later, when the children grew up, the ponies disappeared and the paddock became a simpler version of the tapis vert at Versailles, with mown cross-paths and a formal octet of clipped box in the middle. These have become overgrown and been replaced. So much for the kitchen garden, and its rise in the social scale.

'Another great pro for us were the trees. Near the front door was one of the biggest copper beeches in the country, and in the main garden, four centuries old yew trees grown together into a vast, green and rather lumpish-looking, cottage-loaf shape. On the advice of Peter Coats, compiler of this book, we converted the "loaf", by the addition of simple "windows" and a doorway, into a kind of Beatrix Potter cottage, set around with a low Cotswold-type wall, as can be seen in the picture, and planted with cottagey sorts of flowers. A great embellishment has been a pair of standard mop-headed silver holly trees, which we found in our

86

gardening neighbour and friend Rosemary Verey's temptingly stocked nursery, at nearby Barnsley.

'My husband and I both have strong likes and dislikes among flowers. Likes first: phlox, fritillaries, almost all roses, with a Raubritter, which had the good idea to become a climber, a prime favourite, frilly not upright tulips, ceanothus, especially Puget's Blue and the pink Ceres, and Clematis Perle d'Azur. Dislikes include almost any yellow or orange flowers, lilies – but that is sour grapes, because they won't grow for us'.

Lady Westmorland thinks of her garden as 'an antidote to London, peaceful and relaxing'. She adds, 'I like to keep it a little wild – a typical cottage garden with a touch of Versailles – and, like all gardens today, it must be labour-saving. My husband has a very good eye for architectural detail, like the placing of seats or the proportions of a terrace, and we both only tolerate plants that look and are healthy – unlike us wilting owners. And we like personal touches such as the yew tree cottage, the three terraces (all quite small, in chequer-board brick and stone) and a decorative gate into a neighbouring field in the form of a W, our initial'.

A yew-tree cottage, *left*, devised by the compiler of this book and the owners of Kingsmead, makes an endearing feature. Mop headed silver hollies guard the 'door'. *Below*: Terraces on the garden side of the house make extra sitting-rooms in summer.

The Priory

KEMERTON, NEAR TEWKESBURY

MR PETER AND THE HON MRS HEALING

The Priory, at Kemerton, does not look like a priory at all, though there are ruins of a sixteenth-century religious building in the garden. That, and a vast clipped yew tree were the only ready-made features which Mr and Mrs Peter Healing found when they moved in 48 years ago. But there were obvious possibilities for a garden with a stream on either side and gently sloping ground to the south offering pleasant views.

When he was asked what he aimed at making, Peter Healing answers succinctly, 'A Cornucopia'. He continues, 'Flowers tumbling over each other, borders and small enclosed gardens that would be at their best

A border planted thickly to smother weeds, *right*, in a panoply of gold and green and deep wine-coloured foliage – the faces of Achillea Golden Plate catch the eye, as well as the dark red foliage of Rhus cotinus, the Smoke Tree. A touch of scarlet is given by that real connoisseurs' plant, Lobelia cardinalis. *Below*: The eighteenth-century building of refined proportions stands in a garden which is particularly fascinating for the plantsman.

for two or three months. We wanted parts of the garden to flower as other parts faded, with hellebores, primroses and early bulbs followed by early alpines, then dianthus, philadelphus, old roses, species phlox, lavenders, campanulas and so on'.

All the borders at the Priory are 'colour-grouped', each with a definite colour scheme.

Favourite plants include many of the more unusual herbaceous plants which have both beauty and form. Dislikes are man-made hybrids – 'travesties of beautiful species'. Peter Healing concludes 'Our ambition is to have flowers to enjoy in every season, and I am afraid it is cheating, but we do have an orchid house to fill the winter gap'.

Yet another combination of colours, *opposite*, with blue-green clumps of Ruta graveolens, that most popular plant of today (for best effect, its leaves should be hard pruned back in spring). Other stars in this most successful border are cloudy groups of gypsophila, a telling touch of white phlox, and next to the wooden pillar a towering, many-branched Onopordon acanthium, the Scottish thistle, with white, sharply prickled leaves, a most decorative plant. *Right*: A spectacular group of white phlox, next to misty gypsophila. Peter Healing started life as an interior decorator, so has an expert eye for the blending of colours. *Below*: Two remarkably good, seldom grown plants: a sea holly, eryngium, with small white flower bracts, and sharply toothed leaves, and behind, a rich purple Viticella clematis Royal Velours.

Yew Tree Cottage

AMPNEY ST MARY, GLOUCESTERSHIRE

MRS B. SHUKER AND MISS P. STRANGE

The outstanding feature of the garden at Yew Tree Cottage, is that it might be described as a rock garden, though this part of the garden has been designed with such expertise – and such an artistic eye – that it hardly looks like a conventional rock garden. There are no stones sticking up like 'Do It Yourself' versions of Stonehenge. Yet alpine and other rock plants look completely happy, and present a very attractive picture. The garden was started 20 years ago by Miss Penny Strange, and her mother, Mrs Shuker.

Penny Strange does not think of herself as an 'Alpinist'. Modestly she ranks herself as an amateur 'with an interest in all small plants'.

She feels a garden should have variety: in the pictures on these pages we have concentrated on the parts in which under-stated rocks are becomingly concealed by cushions and carpets of favourite low-growing plants, such as Kabschia and Aizoon saxifrages, Viola cornuta, Erodium chamaedryoides, Coum cyclamen, and the pink-and-white Silene acaulis. Other favourite plants, most of which are lime lovers, which flourish in Penny Strange's perfectly-maintained garden include the fascinating Pasque flowers, Anemone pulsatilla. All present the most unusual and beautiful flowers set in fern-like foliage: A p alpina is pure white; and A p sulphurea shows golden flowers. That great expert on the flora of the Alps. Will Ingwersen, in his classic Manual of Alpine Plants, singles one particular Anemone pulsatilla for the highest praise, A pulsatilla verna, of which he writes, 'This has been acclaimed the most lovely of all alpine flowers . . . low tufts of carroty leaves and short stems, with golden bronze hairs and upturned goblet-shaped flowers, iridescent and opal-white within, with a tassel of golden stamens'.

A fascinating feature of Yew Tree Cottage garden is one that many readers might like to copy. Knowing how difficult to find – and expensive – genuine stone troughs are, Penny Strange describes in four simple steps how she successfully makes her own out of old, white kitchen sinks.

First, paint the sink with the Unibond and water. 2. Make a dry mixture of 2 parts sand, 1 part cement, 1 part peat. 3. Add water to half of the mix to start with, and apply to sink, starting at top corners and working downwards. The coating should be ½-inch thick. Continue inside the sink about 2 inches, and leave to dry. 4. Paint with a mixture of cow manure and milk.

To grow Alpines and rock plants successfully it is essential to have the right soil – equal parts of loam, leaf-mould and sharp sand, with some grit round the necks of the plants that dislike winter wet. Many rock plants like to be cut back after flower to promote new growth. The depth of soil in your trough can be raised by discreet 'building up' with small rocks or pieces of tufa. It sounds a useful tip, and great fun to do.

The small yellow flowered Azorella trifurcata, *opposite above*, with thymes and mossy saxifrages make a rich carpet. As in all well constructed rock gardens, the rocks themselves are barely visible. *Opposite below*: thymes, dianthus and miniature geraniums completely cover the ground, and defy weeds. In the foreground flat growing Cotoneaster congesta spills over on to the gravel. *Above*; low growing plants, in many colours, contrast effectively with gravel and make a pleasing informal edging.

Oare House

PEWSEY, WILTSHIRE

MR HENRY KESWICK AND THE HON MRS KESWICK

A kneeling figure, *left*, of the school of Van Nost offers a sundial to the sun. *Above*: The north façade and front door. A cupola enlivens the otherwise rather sober roofline. *Below*: The southern façade overlooks a spreading lawn running down to the white railings of the swimming pool. On either side, the golden leaves of Frisia pseudoacacia.

I went to Oare House for the first time before the war. At that time it belonged to Sir Geoffrey and Lady Fry and it made a lasting impression on me, as did the Frys' fascinating daughter, now Jennifer Ross. The Frys, with the help of the eminent architect, Clough Williams Ellis, the magician who conjured the fantasy of Portmeirion, had made spectacular additions to what had been a small, early eighteenth-century house, approached by an unexpectedly magnificent avenue of limes. Sir Geoffrey died in 1960, and his widow sold Oare to Sir Alexander Downer, High Commissioner for Australia.

After a few years, the house passed into the hands of the present owner, a keen and imaginative gardener who, with the help of the brilliant Bernard Upton, and his two assistants, Michael Ginning and Karin Rawson, has brought the gardens to their present high pitch of perfection.

But Oare House and garden would look very different today had the Frys and Clough Williams Ellis not exercised their taste and genius upon it. It was they who added the wings on either side of the house, which give it its present dignity, and it was they who created the spreading gardens with their almost Italian vistas, pergolas, high dusky yew hedges and perfectly proportioned elaboration. A photograph I found in an old issue of *Country Life*, taken some 25 years ago, shows the gardens much as they are today.

In 1979, I was asked to simplify and modernise the planting. The Frys' original plan was hardly to be changed at all; nor did I want to do so.

With a generous patron and the inspired Mr Upton and his able helpers, I think the gardens are improved – though chief credit must go to the original planners.

An ironwork gate, *top right*, set in a wall of brick and flint. As this area is partially shaded, the borders on either side are planted with Hosta glauca. *Above*: Beautifully proportioned white ironwork gates. *Below left*: The main herbaceous border as it is now and, *above*, as it was before the lavender hedge was removed, to reveal the bright colours of the informal edging. *Opposite*: A wide swathe of lawn with, at the far end to catch the eye, one of the opulent garden seats, designed by Clough Williams Ellis.

Troy

WALLINGFORD, OXFORDSHIRE

MR AND MRS RUCK-KEENE

The thatched and flint built summer house, *above*, in a setting of thyme planted paving, where Jerome K. Jerome wrote 'Three Men in a Boat'. *Below left*: In spring, a sundial makes the pivotal point in a garden with its ground strewn with many coloured cushions of flowers. *Below right*: The shuttered facade of the house overlooks a garden with high-spirited plantings of different coloured clumps of foliage – presiding, a graceful crimson-leaved Japanese maple. *Opposite*: Until one came to grief in a freak draught, the front terrace was embellished with a graceful pair of snowy Shirotae cherries.

The house at Troy was built in 1827, and is a simple square Regency farmhouse, built of unusual grey-glazed bricks from a local kiln. It was once owned by Jerome K. Jerome, who describes it in his autobiography as 'an old farmhouse on the hill above Wallingford'. In those days, it had two front doors, and he tells how they were used according to which way the wind was blowing. He also mentions the summer house where he did a lot of his writing, including *Three Men in a Boat*, and the yew hedges which still exist. H. G. Wells, W. W. Jacobs and Conan Doyle were among his friends who visited him at Troy. Jerome himself is buried in beautiful Ewelme churchyard some three miles away.

The house and garden were both enlarged about 1926, and there are now about two-and-a-half acres of well-kept flowery pleasure grounds. The soil is neutral and gravelly, so most things grow well, even quite delicate things like a half-hardy creeping Rosemary brought back from Cyprus; and a huge Fremontodendron californicum, which sometimes shows its three-inch across single yellow flowers in mid-November. All cherries thrive, and the surviving Prunus Shirotae still gives shade over the terrace.

A paved terrace is planted with low-growing creeping plants, such as aubretia, alyssum and silver-leaved anaphalis. This terrace is presided over by a handsome old garden seat which might have been designed by Lutyens. When Mr and Mrs Ruck-Keene came to Troy 18 years ago, they were lucky to find another garden seat – an unusual five-sided, white-painted one, made in the Chinese Chippendale manner, which was neatly fitted inside the octagonal gazebo.

The garden at Troy has a much-loved look, and is constantly being changed – the aim always being to save labour. Bedding plants are cut to the minimum and much thought is given to plans and plants that improve with age: stone paths with moss and self-sown seeds; bulbs which multiply grow in tangled profusion of flowers and, of course, shrubs and trees, all of which continue to give pleasure with only the minimum of human help. Birds and butterflies are an added bonus, if a little temptation is provided for them: an old font makes a beautiful bird bath, and sedum and buddleia are planted to attract butterflies. Even a strategic clump of nettles has been left for Peacock butterflies to nest in.

The garden of Troy is not a grand garden, nor, really is it a plantsman's garden, and Mrs Ruck-Keene modestly does not spend a fortune on it, and in return for a small outlay each year, plus a little imagination, some hard work and a lot of patience, they 'think and hope we have achieved a real pleasure garden, a place where we just wanted people to feel happy'.

A seat in the Lutyens style, *above*, and a sundial on the brightly carpeted terrace. *Below left*: A summer border of foxgloves with blue Geranium Endressii at their feet. Johnson's Blue is one of the best herbaceous geraniums. *Below right*: June flowering iris by a brick bordered pool. *Opposite page*: A bow shaped border, brick edged to make for easy mowing, gaily set out with blue pansies, and a kaleidoscope of other brightly coloured flowers.

The Owl House

LAMBERHURST, KENT

MAUREEN, MARCHIONESS OF DUFFERIN AND AVA

Lady Dufferin's country retreat is an enchanting little tile-hung cottage with what must be the crookedest chimney in Kent. When she found it there was hardly the suggestion of a garden: 'an old plum tree in the front and a cabbage patch at the side – that was all'. But a promising asset was a neglected field, bordered on three sides by impenetrable and protective woods.

The former owners were selling to move nearer to London. The price was negotiated and, within a few weeks, she found herself the proud possessor of what turned out to be one of the oldest and most historic buildings in Kent. It is mentioned in the Bodleian Library at Oxford, and its occupant 500 years ago used to pay the monks of nearby Bayham Abbey a yearly rent

of one cockerel. It was the hiding place for wool smugglers who only operated under the cover of night, and so were called 'owlers'. Hence the name of the house today: The Owl House. When the owlers heard the then equivalent of the local police approaching, they warned each other by hooting.

Of her garden, Lady Dufferin says, and rightly, 'Personally I think it is beautiful, and I am proud to have created it. One may be lucky and create a beautiful child, but what comes later? When making a garden and, so to speak, bringing it up to maturity, you can correct any mistakes with the minimum of fuss. And, although it grows up, a garden never leaves you, however ancient you become, it is always there. Whatever is wrong elsewhere, if you have a garden it

A stone owl, *opposite* – what better genius loci for a property called
The Owl House? – surveys a flowery bank of rhododendrons.
Above: The cottage with, in the foreground, Magnolia liliiflora nigra,
with winey purple buds.

A temple *opposite*, wreathed in flowery wisteria. *Above*: A water-baby clasping an outsize frog in a circular lily pond afloat with water lilies and their gleaming pads. *Below*: In spring the wilder parts of the garden are aglow with colour.

ensures the ownership of something lovely and soothing. Instead of dreading the next year, a garden makes such silly thoughts quite impossible. In fact, I am madly impatient for next year to come as quickly as possible to see if all my new plants have been a success: and to enjoy old favourites that will have become that much more established.

'When asked what are my favourite plants, I am always faced with a worrying dilemma. I love literally hundreds of plants, and when I try to list my favourites, I immediately start feeling terribly guilty. I am faced with all those many other favourites, only temporarily forgotten – and straight away want to rewrite my list.

'Real favourites range from the simple cowslip to the magnificent magnolia. Others would certainly include Narcissus cyclamineus, the one like a ballet dancer; the white daffodil Mount Hood, which looks almost transparent in its purity; and those three old friends, daffodils King Alfred, Golden Harvest and Unsurpassable.

'Of all the many lovely camellias surely none is ever quite as beautiful as C williamsii Donation, with its long-flowering, orchid pink flowers.

'If I am ever asked by a visitor to the Owl House gardens to name the particularly beautiful clematis that they have admired, nine times out of ten it will turn out to be Nelly Moser, not one of my own favourites.

'And when the same question is asked of a rhododendron, it is a safe guess that it will be Pink Pearl. It is especially difficult to choose favourites from a large family such as rhododendrons. Two of the standard varieties that I particularly like, unfortunately have unattractive names: Mrs Leake who has large trusses of vivid pink flowers with a purple-brown eye, and Betty Wormald, which is a lovely Pink Pearl hybrid, with enormous trusses of coral-pink flowers, the edges flushed with a deeper pink and starting from crimson buds, giving a splendid effect.

'My favourite azaleas are two of the Japanese Karume hybrids: Hi-No-Digiri, meaning, so I am told, Red Hussar, but which is, in fact, bright crimson; and Hi-No-Mayo, a floriferous soft pink. But of all the beautiful azalea family, I get the greatest pleasure from the occidentalis hybrid, Irene Koster. She has long-tubed, blush-pink and yellow flowers, supported on strong graceful bushes. And she is unique on account of her strong but deliciously delicate fragrance, which may sound Irish, but I am Irish, and it is absolutely descriptive.

'I cannot end without mentioning roses, as I suppose that I love these most of all. I am very lucky in being

able to grow both rhododendrons and roses at the Owl House, and to have the space to go on experimenting with these beauties. One of my favourite roses is Frühlingsgold. Alas, it does not last very long, but it is still a must. No other rose grows quite so gracefully along arched boughs whilst giving out the most intoxicating scent. If possible, I like to see at least two lovely roses and a clematis rambling through every tree.

'I have two Bobbie James ramblers which are far more spectacular than the better-known Kiftsgate. These two, with their far-reaching fragrance, have completely covered two 40-foot silver birch trees with their creamy-white flowers and their beautiful foliage.

'Another special, less well-known rose, is Rose-Marie Viaud of superlative beauty with its amethyst flowers. In my garden it rambles enthusiastically through one of the largest apple trees. I am also very fond of the heavenly pink and fragrant rose Aloha.

'Pet dislikes? I can't bear over-spaced planting in gloomy straight lines. If the same plants were massed together in their separate species, they would probably be worthwhile. I'm also not particularly fond of white chrysanthemums.

'One must be able to find complete peace in a garden. It should be a place where you can go and sit surrounded by beautiful plants and listen to the birds singing. Therefore it is important to have plenty of garden seats, judiciously placed.

'I am deeply grateful for having been able to make a woodland garden which people seem to love. Of course, over the years, there have been disappointments. But one forgets these, the drought, the vandal who broke the stone owl's ear, the even more upsetting vandal, masquerading as a professional gardener. I am not sure of the name for cutting mania, but daffodils were· cut down the day after they flowered, the floribunda roses were pruned around Christmas, and even some of the larger shrubs including the "weeping" varieties were not spared. These setbacks, however, are minor when you consider the intense pleasure the garden gives you and, one hopes, others'.

A suggestion of architectural formality, *opposite*, with the green fields of Kent beyond. *Above*: In a damp dell the exotic lysichitum show their yellow flowers and rich green foliage. Natives of America, their colloquial name there, skunk cabbage, is sometimes almost too apt. *Below*: The golden largesse of spring scatters flowers at the plinth of a classic urn.

Warham House

NEAR WELLS, NORFOLK

MAJOR AND LADY MARY HARVEY

The garden at Warham House, was first laid out in 1959, when the Harveys found a garden with very few interesting plants or trees. One part had been a tennis court, another a chicken run; but there were good walls on three sides which provided much-needed shelter from frequent north-east winds. The soil was light and alkaline, no good for rhododendrons or azaleas, but just right for Mediterranean plants which like sea salt in the air, and for grey-leaved plants which are favourites, as well as useful shrubs such as philadelphus, viburnum, hypericum and potentillas. Hostas, invaluable for their good-natured disposition and luxuriant summer foliage, are happy. Roses do not take kindly to the soil, and have to be cosseted, to which they gratefully respond.

The visitor to the garden at Warham House is immediately aware that much thought and knowledge has gone into the arrangement of the planting. Good foliage has been given as much consideration as a show of flowers. Bold clumps of plants with silver-grey or red foliage have been interspersed with bold clumps of brightly coloured flowers, always a sign of good garden arrangement. A few such combinations that take the eye effectively are silvery ballota near purple-leaved Cotinus Royal Purple, the different greens and textures of Sedum spectabile, alchemilla and Bergenia cordifolia – the last two unrivalled as ground covers. Nearby, against a hedge of rich copper beech, the creamy leaves of Cornus sibirica stand out in striking contrast.

It is plantings such as this, that make a visit to the garden at Warham well worthwhile.

A feature added in 1965 was the summer house, designed by Fletcher Watson, which acts as an effective eye-catcher at the end of the raised herbaceous borders.

The herbaceous borders, *opposite*, are raised and closely planted to save weeding. *Above left*: By the garden door, giving on to a neatly paved terrace, grows a vigorous pyracantha, covered with white flowers in spring, to the delight of bees, and berries in the autumn. *Above right*: Bright geraniums and Cineraria maritima with its silver leaves in a swagged stone urn, at the entrance to the herbaceous border garden, with, as 'eye-catcher' – a conically-roofed summer house.

Sedgebrook Manor

LINCOLNSHIRE

THE HON JAMES AND LADY CAROLINE OGILVY

The newly created lake, *left*, with silver-barked birches looking at their reflections in the water, and the deep colour of moisture-loving Iris sibirica. *Above*: The Thorold shield over the door. *Below right*: A summer house half-roofed with honeysuckle.

Sedgebrook Manor lies in a part of England enriched with telling features. The Vale of Belvoir is nearby, and the spreading fertile acres bordering the Trent. The house itself has a long history. Once it was the home of the Markham family – of which one member became Chief Justice to Edward IV. In the early eighteenth century it was brought by the Thorolds, a family going back to before the Conquest, and it is the Thorold shield we see carved over the classically sculpted front door. The present owners are Lady Caroline and the Hon James Ogilvy, and today a smiling garden lies round the grey stone walls of their home. The garden was originally made in 1931, after a long period during which the Manor had been used as a farmhouse. Lady Caroline found good lawns, hedges, not one but two large vegetable gardens, and a rose garden with an unfortunate mixture of roses in each small bed.

Lady Caroline's aim was to 'have something to look at from the windows of the house', from which there

An eighteenth-century gardener, *opposite*, one of a pair, and possibly by Van Nost. *Above*: A hedged enclosure close carpeted with petunias. *Below*: Close planting defeats weeds. *Below right*: A golden cushion of spicily scented origanum.

are no extensive views. Her favourite flowers are roses, and after that, all the flowers of spring such as snowdrops, daffodils, bluebells and tulips. 'The Switzers of our guard' as Andrew Marvell described them, in such military ranks were they planted in the seventeenth century. At Sedgebrook, tulips and indeed most other flowers, are planted less strictly and there is a heartening informality about the garden in spite of a splendid pair of statues, which embellish one hedged enclosure. These figures, such is the perfection of their lines, could be the work of the celebrated Van Nost, whose work yard was at Hyde Park Corner, a quieter location in the seventeenth century than now. Another touch of formality is to be found in the entrance forecourt, where there is a good example of how well-tailored evergreens can add style and character to a garden. Here, as can be seen in the picture, the twin genii loci are a perfectly matched pair of, not high-stepping bays, but high-growing Irish yews.

Lady Caroline thought that a fault in her garden was that it lacked water, so she took advantage of the very dry summer of 1976 to create an attractive *pièce d'eau*. The area was naturally boggy, but during that torrid, rainless summer, it was caked as hard as brick, which made the work easier – though it took several years before the little lake took on the attractive look it has today – with soaring silver birches admiring their white stems in the water. The edges of the lake are allowed to stay wild, with buttercups and natural reeds, and some bold clumps of blue Iris sibirica.

There is no lack of colour in the garden at Sedgebrook. Each of the differently hedged enclosures has a character and features of its own. One has a summer house, draped with a sensational honeysuckle "Greta," and white clematis; another has a ground-covering in summer of a close carpet of petunias. A herb garden is brightened every spring with brilliant cushions of origanum.

Fryerning House

INGATESTONE, ESSEX

MR AND MRS KEITH BROWN

When Mr and Mrs Gore-Browne bought Fryerning House near Ingatestone, in Essex, soon after the war, the garden looked very different, but they soon recognised its possibilities. The soil was acid, so they knew that azaleas and rhododendrons would grow well for them, and there were drifts of the sweet-smelling Azalea mollis in the wood which bordered the garden. But the garden did not have any very remarkable ready-made features.

The long borders stretched from the garden door to a low wall. There were rose beds in the centre and a pergola down one side of the garden. The rose beds were done away with, and a new rose garden put elsewhere. The pergola was scrapped: years afterwards, Mr and Mrs Gore-Browne sometimes wondered if this had not been a mistake. But there were good trees – a fine weeping willow in particular – and the setting was beautiful, with the wood to the west of the garden; and above all, the acid soil.

Borders were created on the far side of the low wall, and planted with shrub roses, species rhododendrons and foliage plants. More trees were planted to give shelter from the prevailing south-west wind. (Trees and shrubs that were of special interest in the garden at Fryerning were, and one hopes still are: Nyssa sylvatica, Acer Hersii, with its beautiful marbled bark, Acer Osakasuki and, for autumn colour, Fothergilla monticola.) Masses of peat was dug into the heavy, gravelly soil to lighten it. A new rosé garden was made on the east side of the garden. (Many experienced gardeners are of the opinion that exposure to a sharp east wind is of great benefit to roses, as it blows away pests such as greenfly and reduces mildew.) The planting of the wood was elaborated, and the Azalea mollis soon had for neighbours such rare and interesting rhododendrons as the scarlet Fabia, the sulphur yellow Hawk/Crest, the red, black-rayed Romany Chai – its odd name means Gypsy children – and the Himalayan

A border, *opposite*, which owes much of its sparkle to the inclusion of
the silver and grey foliage of lavender and santolina.
Above: The windows of the house overlook a flower filled garden.

species Thompsonii, a most generous flowerer, and Yakusimanum.

A feature of the planting in the garden at Fryerning, which was everywhere apparent, was the use of grey, gold and evergreen foliage plants to set off the colour of more transient flowers. More about that later.

Favourite roses were the floribunda Ballerina, with its generous sprays of small pink flowers, both the red and pink Garnette (invaluable for their long-lasting qualities when cut), the yellow Chinatown, Elizabeth of Glamis, Plentiful and Dearest.

In the summer, an effective feature of the garden is the pair of borders by the terrace in front of the house – important, as they are always in view. These borders were planted with roses, lavender, different fuchsias, heathers, doryncnium, the golden-leaved Meadowsweet, Filipendula ulmaria aurea, eryngium and silver-leaved artemisias, especially effective if next to a red-leaved berberis. But another word about silver foliage. No garden fashion – and there are fashions in gardening, just as there are in dressing – has so quickly become popular than the prevalent taste for plants of silver and grey foliage. Gertrude Jekyll started it, as she did so many good things, years ago, and immediately the knowing few, the devotees of her articles in *Country Life* and of her books, which had yet to become classics, followed her lead. Almost overnight silver-leaved plants played an important role in gardening, and continue to do so today.

Of a special corner of her garden, Miss Jekyll herself wrote: 'Suddenly turning to look into the "grey" garden, the effect is surprising, quite astonishingly luminous and refreshing – not only in itself, but for the contrast that grey and silver-leaved plants provide for coloured flowers. One never knew how vividly bright ageratum could be – or lavender or nepeta – the purple of the clematis of the Jackmanii type becoming piercingly brilliant'.

Grey and silver foliage is not only alluring in itself, but, as the great Gertrude pointed out, it makes a perfect foil for more brightly coloured leaves of other plants. So, in the borders at Fryerning, the use of many 'silvers' and thoughtfully chosen other plants makes a tapestry of softly blended colours for months on end. Even in winter, the different forms and foliages make a warm tortoiseshell pattern which is cheerful on the darkest days.

The new owners of Fryerning are Mr and Mrs Keith Brown, for whom one of its great attractions was the garden. It is good to know that it will continue to be well maintained – and, in short, cherished.

More touches of silver, *opposite*, in a closely planted border with cushions of different colours, in symmetrical but informal style. *Above*: Changing the colour scheme with the lavish use of Calluna vulgaris Golden Hope to introduce more sunset tones and shades of warmer brown. *Below*: It is extraordinary how much garden colour can be conjured by the use, as here, of different leaf colours, with only a few clumps of flower.

118

Bledlow Manor

NEAR AYLESBURY, BUCKINGHAMSHIRE
LORD AND LADY CARRINGTON

Few people in Britain have a more demanding life than Lord Carrington, but fortunately he has an uncommonly restful home awaiting him at the end of his frequent journeys.

When the Carringtons moved into Bledlow Manor 37 years ago, there was little garden to speak of. But there were one or two promising features; a 500-year-old yew, box hedges, and old walls enclosing large areas of nettles and weeds.

Robert Adams, a landscape architect who had worked in Greece and the Middle East, as well as Britain, was consulted. He found the project 'a wonderful opportunity to attempt to create a garden which reflected the style of the manor and complemen-ted it'. He takes as a compliment the care and main-tenance that the garden has subsequently been given.

The garden today is a happy blend of formality – to match the formality of the house – and a series of self-contained gardens enclosed in walls or hedges, each with its own character, and each planted very much in the taste of the present day.

Plants that thrive on the chalky soil of the garden include Viburnums (including the standard V carlesii – a special favourite), lilacs, lavender and dianthus. Hybrid Tea Roses are less successful, and azaleas impossible.

But for months in the summer, the garden is full of colour – to the brim.

A curved mixed border, *opposite*, with golden origanum (marjoram) in the foreground, leads the eye to a rich border of old roses. *Opposite below left*: old fashioned English border flowers such as Stachys lanata and Sweet William make a pattern of bright colours. *Opposite below right*: Over the garden wall lies a park-like field. *Below left*: A statue of St Peter presides over a triangular garden with low box hedges containing panels of low growing silvery plants such as anaphalis and stachys. Lord Carrington (christian name Peter) acquired the statue, when repairs were being carried out on the south west tower of the Palace of Westminster. *Below right*: The garden façade seen beyond the rose garden with well furnished beds of the yellow floribunda rose Korresia, golden William Bell, white Iceberg and Blanc Double de Coubert.

Sherbourne Park

WARWICKSHIRE

MR CHARLES AND THE HON MRS SMITH-RYLAND

A great garden expert once wrote that the well-designed garden should consist of a bold overall pattern of paths, walls and hedges, but the planting these features contain should be allowed a degree of informality. Hedges should be meticulously clipped, but the plants they contain should, in contrast, not be too rigidly aligned. Paths should be weed-free and, if of gravel, kept well raked, but the plants on either side should be permitted to lap over the edges, to create an informal swathe of different soft colours. Pots and urns do not have to be filled with geraniums alone, effective as such a planting can be. A mixture can be very attractive as, for example, shown on page 123. Low walls can look rather stark if not curtained with overhanging plants to soften the edges. Sherbourne Park is full of examples of such thoughtful planting.

The house dates from 1730 and its architect is said to have been Smith of Warwick. It lies three miles to the south of Warwick, and has been in the Smith-Ryland family for 150 years. Charles Smith-Ryland is Lord Lieutenant of Warwickshire.

When Mrs Smith-Ryland started work on the garden in 1959, she found little enough to go on. All the ready-made amenities that she remembers are two lawns bisected by gravel paths, four malus and some clumps of Pampas grass. Her aim was to make a garden which contained some surprises and unexpected corners, but she realised that the 'bones' had to be carefully planned before she embarked on any 'frills'.

Of all the flowers that grow in the garden at Sherbourne Park, summer-flowering jasmines are prime favourites, though all scented flowers are preferred; roses and lilies, for instance, and philadelphus, to tulips or iris. The soil of the garden is too light for Hybrid Tea roses though Floribundas and the 'old-fashioned' species roses do well.

The garden with its very English charm, combined with perfect taste in planting and touches of almost Gallic elegance, *vaut bien la visite*. It is open regularly for various good causes.

A shepherdess, *opposite*, in lead, is separated by an ironwork door from her gentleman friend. *This page left*: At her feet hellebores and euphorbia, at his, Bergenia cordifolia. *This page right*: A low wall grown over with the branches of Mahonia japonica, and edged with a froth of Alchemilla mollis.

The rose garden, *opposite*, at Sherbourne Park with its diamond-shaped beds, edged with box. This page, *above left and right*, one of the several brick walls in the garden hung with bright variegated ivy Gloire de Marengo. *Right*: A comparitive newcomer to English gardens, Fremontodendron californicum, shows itself quite at home in cooler Warwickshire. *Left*: A brilliant example of the well-filled container of which the planting is in perfect proportion to an old stone urn. *Below right*: Fuchsias make ideal pot plants for a terrace, with a lead peacock as genius loci.

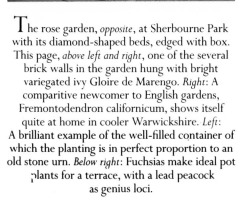

The Forge House

EAST HADDON, NORTHAMPTONSHIRE

MR AND MRS ROBERT BARROW

When Mr and Mrs Bob Barrow bought their house in a Northamptonshire village, just over 25 years ago, neither of them knew much about the technicalities of gardening. So they had the good idea of planning their garden as they would a house – with a series of rooms leading into each other. 'We used balustrades and pergolas as walls', says Bob Barrow. 'Clematis, honeysuckle, wisteria, ivy, roses and conifers as wallpaper – and numerous urns, finials and statuary as furniture.

'An elevated sun terrace overlooking the swimming-pool was made with the "back-fill" of the pool itself, which is now enclosed by a high balustrade thickly curtained with Clematis montana. Swimming-pools are so seldom beautiful to look at, but I think ours has been much improved be being given a Roman bath atmosphere, surrounded by 22 Tuscan columns, half covered with carefully trained climbers. A bust of Bacchus presides at one end, and seems quite happy to watch our antics in the pool, as he is smiling broadly.

'What we call our Islamic garden is surrounded on three sides by a densely planted hedge of that excellent

A spectacular dracaena, *opposite*, makes an explosion of leaves against a blue patch of Northamptonshire sky. *Below*: Vases of stone fruit and flowers stand on either side of steps leading up to the 'Islamic' garden.

floribunda rose, The Fairy, listed in most books as 'dwarf' but so happy does it appear in our Northamptonshire clay that it seems to have overcome its dwarfish habit, and made a respectable hedge. In the centre of this garden is an imposing stone vase – 12-sided with rhythmical horseshoe arches and hexagonal decoration. Other stone vases are decorated with carved Ashoka bud decoration – all of which recalls, if somewhat freely, a garden planned by the Moors in sun-soaked Granada.

'Our soil, though good for roses is definitely alkaline – so, of course, no azaleas or rhododendrons. Camellias are hard work, but survive if dosed liberally with life-giving Sequestrine. All conifers do well, and in the early summer, the air is heavy with the scent of Viburnum burkwoodii and Lonicera tellmanniana. In June, shrub roses, such as Roseraie de l'Hay and Tuscany come into their own; these have replaced the herbaceous border which we found when we came to The Forge House, and which had got completely out of control'.

Bob Barrow continues, 'We have furnished our garden with urns, jardinières and troughs, all planted differently. Many of these, of course, come from the Haddonstone collection, our own firm, which we operate next door'.

Overall, ancient and benign, presides the tower of St Mary's Church, with its twelfth-century carvings.

The 'Islamic' garden, *opposite*, is enclosed with a hedge of that long flowering rose, The Fairy. In the centre stands a carved stone centre-piece. In the background rises the sturdy tower of St Mary's Church. *This page*: The garden of the Forge House, as might be expected, is effectively furnished with some of the stone objects for which Mr Barrow's firm 'Haddonstone' is famous. Urns, balustrades, benches or sundials are all displayed, among the flowers, to the very best advantage.

Capel Manor

ENFIELD, MIDDLESEX

Lancelot Brown, the famous eighteenth-century landscapist, would always say, when asked to advise on any site, 'Let us first consider its capabilities'. What are the capabilities of Capel Manor?

The great Lancelot would find little to do there, as the small but beautifully planned grounds were landscaped, and by a master hand, years ago.

Why, then 'capabilities'? Because, at Capel Manor, there is the Institute of Horticulture, which is able to offer several valuable courses of different kinds, for would-be gardeners, both amateur and professional.

The Institute has an important site in which to offer these facilities: the old estate of 30 acres, lying around Capel Manor.

Capel Manor, once the property of the Medcalf family, is surrounded by an old-fashioned garden – largely replanted in the past seven years – complete with brick walls, greenhouses and, best of all, some magnificent old trees, including the tallest Copper Beech in the country, and over 200 years old; other interesting trees are good specimens of the Turner Oak (Quercus X Turneri): this is semi-evergreen, in that it retains its old leaves until the new growth replaces them in spring. Another interesting tree is a kind of elm, Zelkova carpinifolia – the second tallest in England: Zelkova was imported from the Caucasus in 1760. At one time it was thought to be one of the few members of the elm family which was immune from Dutch elm disease but, unfortunately, this has proved not to be the case.

A tree in the garden at Capel Manor which always attracts attention is the Tulip Tree, Liriodendron tulipifera. It acquired its colloquial name because its flowers (also the shape of its leaves) strongly resemble the flowers of a tulip.

The garden at Capel Manor is primarily a garden of instruction. But, like many of the best planned and thought-out gardens of today, such as Sissinghurst and

A paved path, *opposite*, is bordered by a flower bed, planted in an unusual combination of Ricinus communis Gibsonii, the Castor Oil plant, with its wine-dark leaves, alongside low growing white nicotianas, with the red flowered variety Idol in front. *Above*: 'I only tell of sunny hours', an apt quotation, for any sundial. Beyond grows golden-leaved Frisia pseudoacacia.

Hidcote Manor, it is divided into sections, each devoted to a certain type of plant, or to plants which are at their best at a special season. In a garden planned for the study of horticulture this is a particularly practical, as well as interesting, arrangement. There is a pool garden, a woodland area, a walled garden and several enclosed gardens. Each has its special planting and character.

Shrubs play an important part in the planting, for they are both labour- and space-saving: important qualities in the more modestly proportioned gardens of today.

Among the interesting shrubs and smaller trees seen in the garden of Capel Manor are many magnolias underplanted with a ground cover of hardy geraniums. In another part of the garden is an important collection of cotoneasters 'grouped together to help with comparison and identification'.

Sorbus of different varieties are much in evidence – two, especially, the feathery-leaved Sorbus Joseph Rock, and conradinae, of which the fastigiate narrow habit of growth enables it to be planted where there would be no room for a more widely spreading tree.

In a short space, it is difficult to enumerate all the points of interest in the garden at Capel Manor. But any visitor, especially if he is something of a plantsman, will find a great deal here which will interest him.

The garden has been planted not only for the specialist, but also for particular sections of the general public. For instance, there is a special area for the physically disabled, with an octagonal greenhouse specially adapted for the use of people in wheelchairs.

The Capel Manor Institute of Horticulture, maintained and administered by the Education Committee of the London Borough of Enfield, is open to the public some eleven days between April and September. It well repays a visit.

A massed bank, *opposite*, of many coloured annuals adds brightness in late summer. *Below*: A pergola is a feature of the garden at Capel Manor, and is hung in summer with baskets of pink geraniums and silver-leaved helichrysum.

Crucks

GREAT HASELEY, OXFORDSHIRE

MRS LEONARD BARNES

The bright torches of Red Hot poker, Kniphofia uvaria, *left*, light up a corner of Mrs Barnes' garden. In the background the conical roofed garden room for Mrs Barnes' late erudite husband to work in. *Below*: the fifteenth-century house.

When Mr and Mrs Barnes found their fifteenth-century house, Crucks, at Great Haseley, there were few ready-made garden features, except one beautiful lime tree 'growing out of a rich mulch of builders' rubble'. However, fortunately, there seemed to be a few deep-rooted weeds. The site for the garden was not an easy one, as the house was tucked in at one end, and any formal plan presented difficulties. The final decision was to have curved borders round the boundaries on two sides and fill them with shrub roses, and only a few carefully chosen herbaceous plants; all the rest would be lawn. On the sunny side, a paved terrace was laid, carpeted here and there with deep purple flowered thyme (Thymus serpyllum).

In 1969, a summer house for Mr Barnes, a distinguished don at Oxford, to work in, was added. Tall shrubs at the back of the borders provided privacy.

Mrs Barnes realises the value of plants which give value all the year round, so yew and box are much in evidence, as are four cypresses on the street side of the garden. Another favourite planting plan is contrasting habits of growth – the spires of foxgloves, for instance, against the rounded form of shrub roses, rising above peonies. Walls are curtained in clematis, and Mrs Barnes is careful to choose – to save labour – 'kinds that are cut down in February, as the early flowerers get too untidy'. Wooden fences were smothered with roses, honeysuckles and different ivies so that they become half fence and half hedge – what that great gardener, Clarence Elliott, used to call 'fedges'.

Daffodils and tulips are followed by the invaluable Alstroemeria Ligtu, which effectively covers the space left by the deceased spring bulbs. (Other plants which do this most effectively are the large-leaved hostas, such as glauca and Sieboldii.)

Special dislikes, at Crucks, are stridently coloured modern roses such as Super Star, mini-lily ponds and almost any kind of rockery.

Mrs Barnes is lucky in her soil, and her garden enjoys rich loam. A Magnolia Goliath she planted herself has lived up to its name, being already a specimen tree and, incidentally, entirely trouble-free.

So many people hesitate to plant magnolias, surely one of 'the noblest of all flowering trees', as the great Vita Sackville-West called them, fearing that they are too slow growing. They might well try Goliath.

'If I can be described', says Mrs Barnes, 'as having a garden philosophy, it is to try always to have something, somewhere, showing a little colour, but not to attempt to have colour everywhere all the time'.

A magnificent specimen, *above left*, of one of the most impressive of euphorbias E Wulfenii (with every quality except an occasional rather unpleasant foxy smell). *Right*: The summer house walls are curtained in different large flowered clematis, such as the rich mauve Lasurstern and Etoile Violette. *Opposite*: The sun-catching terrace of thyme carpeted, and time coloured, paving stones.

Rodmarton Manor

GLOUCESTERSHIRE

MRS ANTHONY BIDDULPH

The manor of Rodmarton lies among the green fields of Gloucestershire, a county of beautiful gardens. The great Vita Sackville-West much admired its 'long cool façade looking over an enchanting garden'. Though in traditional Cotswold style, the house is comparatively modern, having been built only 70-odd years ago. The architect was Ernest Barnsley who, with his brother Sidney, did so much to revive the art of Cotswold craftsmanship. Ernest is certainly thought to have been influential in the layout of the garden, aided by the late Mrs Claud Biddulph. This was the moment when Gertrude Jekyll was at the height of her powers, and the garden today, devotedly looked after by the present owner, Mrs Anthony Biddulph, daughter-in-law of the builder of Rodmarton Manor itself, still gives a strong impression of Jekyll influences, rather than of those fashionable trends of today, so widely indulged in as already to have become clichés. Silver foliage here and there, there certainly is, but not to excess; and the popular hallmarks of up-to-the-moment gardening tricks so often shown in the glossy pages of smart magazines (*House & Garden* included), are noticeably absent. Mrs Biddulph's aim was to create an interesting garden, with topiary, bulbs and ground cover, and, of course, it had to be labour-saving. She tries to keep abreast of all innovations – for example, mist sprayer, plastic cloches and electric hedge trimmers. Her aim, in essence, was to make a present-day garden in keeping with the traditional house. Certainly, to the visitor, the garden at Rodmarton has retained its flavour of a garden of before the 1914-18 war, and seems to encapsulate the careful grace of those leisured days.

Up-to-date, labour-saving plantings, so essential today are certainly not neglected. Weed-suppressing plants such as hostas, potentillas and lavender do their good work, and there is no lack of undemanding shrub roses, so often called 'old-fashioned' in spite of the fact that few are more than a century old. Blanc Double de Coubert, the 'old-fashioned rose' par excellence, was only introduced in 1892, and Centenaire de Lourdes, a

A seldom grown rose, *opposite*, with mauve flowers, as its
German name Veilchenblau implies, prettily curtains
an outhouse door. *Above*: The traditional Cotswold face
of Rodmarton Manor rises beyond closely clipped topiary.

favourite of the great rosomane, the late Vicomte de Noailles, only appeared 30 years ago; Cuisse de Nymphe Emue, whose name so excited Vita Sackville-West, is an exception, having been recorded in 1638 when Cardinal Richelieu – after whom another rose was named, but only in 1840 – was all-powerful in France. These are the sort of shrub roses that Mrs Biddulph grows in rough grass – a device which is both picturesque and easy to maintain.

When asked whether she has any special gardening dislikes or rules she replies: 'Yes, snobby gardeners who don't like some shrubs or plants because everyone else has them, "Leylandii", for example, excellent in the right place. As for rules, I think there are five quite important ones: one, if a plant does not do well in one place, try it immediately somewhere else; two, take cuttings of all doubtful doers; three, do not envy rhododendrons and azaleas when you have the wrong soil for them – cherish what you can have; four, feed, feed and feed again, especially if you garden, as I do, on lime soil; five, give away as much as you can – one's garden should be filled with exchanges'.

Today the garden at Rodmarton is specially full of charm. Flower-filled enclosures are planted with such favourites as the giant snowdrop, galanthus, which flowers so long, hellebores and Tree Peonies, and nerines do well. These enclosures adjoin areas of simple paving. On the terrace grow trees of topiary, of which the perfectly clipped, but totally artificial, forms divert and please us, though they would surely have incurred the indignation of Joseph Addison, who once wrote in *The Spectator*: 'Our trees rise in cones and pyramids – we see the work of scissors on every plant and bush . . .' But, forgetting the great satirist's quirks, the visitor to the garden at Rodmarton could find no better place in which to relax for an hour or two, enjoying the scents, the distant views towards the Marlborough Downs, and the sense of serenity which is all pervasive.

A welcoming summer house, *opposite and above*, fits snugly between two well tailored evergreen hedges. *Below*: The strange archaic forms of topiary trees, outlined against a distant view of Gloucestershire pastures. *Above right*: A group of plants in pots – hydrangeas, geraniums, even a datura – cluster by the front door. *Right*: One of the best of all coloured leaved shrubs, Lonicera Baggesens Gold, keeps its rich colour all year round.

Ardleigh Park

NEAR COLCHESTER, ESSEX

MR AND MRS ALFRED ELBRICK

When Colonel and Mrs Judd, until recently the owners of Ardleigh Park, moved to Ardleigh the property had been a riding school and the grounds were completely devastated. Only a few trees remained of the Victorian garden. When they planned the new garden their aim was to make the traditional English garden but with classical undertones. One part of the garden was given an Italian air with clipped beech hedges, with niches for statuary against a background of lime trees which, in 20 years, have reached a height of 30 feet. The swimming-pool was sited in an enclosure with walls on the north and east sides, very important in draughty Essex, and further protected by cypresses, grown from seed, collected from the Mediterranean.

A paved garden was planted with old roses and clumps of yuccas, which seem surprisingly, to thrive in chilly climes so far removed from their Mexican origins. A circular garden was furnished with that best of rugosas, R Blanc Double de Coubert – and a lime walk planted to form an *allée couverte*. All these different areas, which make the garden sound much larger than it is, lead from one to another, with statues introduced at strategic places.

For the new occupants of Ardleigh, Mr and Mrs Elbrick, the garden was an important attraction, so it is pleasant to know that the garden is in such good hands and will surely be cherished, with American zest, good taste and enthusiasm.

Conifers and evergreens, *opposite*, provide a tapestry of different greens all the year round. *Above left*: Reflection in an azure pool. The statue is grown around with golden leaved, white flowered feverfew (Chrysanthemum parthenium). *Right*: Architectural features and tapering conifers complement each other.

Basildon Park

PANGBOURNE, BERKSHIRE
LORD AND LADY ILIFFE

Basildon Park, built between 1776 and 1778 by the celebrated architect, John Carr of York, presents its mellow Bath stone face to the sunshine and shadows of a beautiful part of the Thames Valley. It is set in lush parkland, studded with old trees, survivors of more opulent days.

In 1952, when Lord and Lady Iliffe – and later the National Trust – took over the property, the house had not been lived in since 1911. As Lady Iliffe recounts, 'It had been a convalescent home in the First World War, and had been occupied by the army in the Second. The garden was a wilderness; one could not tell where it began or ended. Here and there we found headless statues lying in beds of nettles'.

Lord and Lady Iliffe, because of the post-war difficulties, aimed at making a small garden, but in scale with the house, which is definitely large. Simplicity of design and planting was of utmost importance, with nothing fussy which would not have suited the lofty, classical walls of the house. Shrub roses were chosen rather than Hybrid Teas. Thus, old roses are favourites, for Lady Iliffe holds that their loose-growing habit, suit the garden, which merges into the park.

'When we started on the garden', Lady Iliffe goes on,

A shady courtyard, *right*, offers a cool home to plants allergic to full sun. *Below left*: A bland façade of one of the wings surveys well planted beds of flowers. *Below right*: Nevada, one of the best of all white or cream coloured roses, below the honey coloured walls of Basildon.

'which I think of as my particular domain, Lanning Roper gave us some Alchemilla mollis, and since then we have never looked back; it has almost taken over in the patio. Lavender does very well; we clip it back at the end of the summer to make umpteen lavender sachets for the Red Cross sale. Philadelphus, all sorts of varieties, but Belle Etoile specially, for scent and because the flowers don't all bloom together.

'My own dislikes include yellow marigolds, bedded-out geraniums, and Michaelmas Daisies, especially the ones that get mildew. I am not mad about yellow flowers in any case, but some have their uses as they show up at night. Daisy Fellowes (a famous and beautiful hostess in the 'thirties and 'forties) once said to me, "If you dine outside, plant white, nothing else shows up". But pale yellow does'.

The garden suffers from poor, shallow soil, and is too well drained, being alkaline over chalk and granite. Most plants benefit from being 'puddled in' with plenty of manure and mulched every year. The aim is to plant as close as possible never leaving bare earth, if possible, to discourage weeds which blow in from the park and surrounding fields.

But old roses will always be the favourites, and Lady Iliffe lists a few of her special ones: Madame Isaac Pereire, for scent which fills the rooms when cut and also as the basis of pot-pourri; the Alchemist, a marvellous apricot and cream variety which, if grown as a shrub, needs support as it over-flowers itself, becomes too heavy and flops to the ground; Roseraie de l'Hay, for its scent, shape, nice leaves and hips later on; the pale pink of Fantin Latour, lifted by strong colour, with its lovely flower shape and scent – 'so nice I can't make myself pick it', says Lady Iliffe; 'Iceberg', that almost too popular white rose, which flowers forever; Aloha, a new discovery with glorious strong, pink flowers; Fritz Nobis with its charming way of growing tall, and then bending down its top for you to look at; Frau Dagmar Hastrup a Rugosa, useful as it keeps its leaves, and makes a handsome, dense bush, with single, pale-pink flowers, and splendid hips; and Charles de Mills for its marvellous dark-red, velvet colour.

Lady Iliffe does not include that favourite old French rose, Madame Ernest Calvat, once so exuberantly described by that great rosarian of the 'twenties and 'thirties, Miss Nancy Lindsay, who lived near Basildon: 'an august bush with young shoots, sparkling rose and violet, and vintage leaves of silver lustred peacock green illuminated carmine: its sumptuous perfumed cabbages are Thyrrhian rose mellowing to seraphic mauve'. Irresistible, surely?

Seen from an upper window, *opposite*, a giant rosette of dwarf roses and lavender. *Above*: A classic urn in a flowery setting. *Below*: Frau Dagmar Hastrup has single flowers, followed by spectacular hips.

Clouds Hill

HITCHIN, HERTFORDSHIRE

LADY LLOYD

In one of the twin borders, *left*, care has been taken to keep variety of leaf and plant form. In the foreground, the white leaves of stachys reflect the sun-catching white façade of the house. *Below*: The main garden path is aligned with an ancient oak tree.

These pictures, and the one on the previous page, were taken at Clouds Hill, in Hertfordshire, where the garden was created 40-odd years ago, out of 'a rough field full of pheasants' nests, by Lady Lloyd, wife of the great Lord Lloyd, Proconsul and ruler of Egypt in the distant years of British power in the Middle East. Though it certainly was Lord Lloyd who, with military precision, devised and placed the crisp, white picket fence and gate which is such a feature of the north side of Clouds Hill, it was his wife and the present Lady Lloyd, keen and knowledgeable gardeners, who created the luxuriant garden as it is today.

Vistas were cut through some of the surrounding woods to make the most of distant views of the Barton

Hills. More recently – in the 'fifties and 'sixties – hedges and borders were planned and planted, and are still meticulously kept up to standard by the present Lady Lloyd.

But several charming new features have been added like generous, bow-shaped terraces in front of the house, on the south-facing side, which provide extra sitting out space. The herbaceous borders are now planted very much in the modern taste, with shrubs to give body and character even in deep winter; and the rose garden is set out with the best of the Hybrid teas of today, such as the brilliant Edward Morse, the ever-popular Peace, Polly, and the richly-scented Shot Silk.

In front of the low, white painted house, 'once a tumble-down vicarage', the genius loci is a magnificent oak, fully 400 years old, upon which the herbaceous borders are aligned.

Although the doughtiest genius loci of the Lloyd's garden is this ancient oak tree, two other genii hardly less doughty, must certainly be mentioned here: Mr Bithrey, the most efficient of gardeners, and Mr Wright, butler and part-time gardener, lawn-mower-in-chief and half-a-dozen other useful things.

The white picket fence, *opposite*, devised and placed by the great Lord Lloyd with military precision. *Above*: Of the hybrid clematis, Nelly Moser is one of the most free flowering. *Below*: Herbaceous borders are planted so that groups of flowers on either side reflect each other.

Palmers Farm

NEAR TUNBRIDGE WELLS, KENT

MRS MERLIN PENNINK

Palmers Farm would be many people's idea of a dream house, and the garden is a great tribute to the talents of its owner.

Ambitious girls working in over-heated city offices, soldiers shivering in the Falklands, up-and-coming business boys who could not resist the temptation of an inflated salary in, say, the business quarter of Miami, where the vegetation consists of plants of the texture of linoleum – all must surely dream of living, some day, in a house like Mrs Pennink's converted farmhouse.

Mrs Pennink is very lucky to own Palmers Farm, and her house is lucky in such an owner, a decorator of perfect but under-stated taste, and a flower arranger par excellence, who seems inspired by Van Huysum.

The garden links the main house, converted barn and nearby cottage, and Mrs Pennink's favourite flowers reflect her special skills. Crown Imperials, Parrot Tulips and old-fashioned roses are all favourites, as are plants of rich and contrasting foliage such as euphorbias and hostas. Mrs Pennink does not agree with Francis Bacon who approved of fountains, but thought 'pools mar all, and make the garden unwholesome and full of flies and frogs'. At Palmers Farm a clear and glistening dew pond reflects the Kentish sky, and in summer is afloat with lilies. But no swimming-pool here, so blue as to rasp the retina, such as one would find, for example, in every Californian suburb.

The garden, with its luscious and labour-saving planting, is in complete sympathy with the fields and woods which are its setting.

A paved path, *opposite*, wends its way through beds of spring flowers. *Above left*: Spring blossom swags a black clapboard gable – in the foreground the different greens and golds of young leaved shrubs make a glistening spring wreath of fresh verdure. *Right*: Veronica spicata is massed on either side of the path to greet, with its pale blue spires, the arriving guest.

The farm, *left*, with its reflecting dew pool and lush planting. Mrs Pennink does not agree with Francis Bacon who thought that 'pools mar all'. *Above*: Mrs Pennink loves to arrange flowers and has a recognized talent for that gentle art. *Below*: The view from the terrace.

Tudor House

THE PARK DEPARTMENT
OF SOUTHAMPTON

The garden, *opposite*, seen through an ancient stone arch, part of the original city wall of Southampton. *Above:* Interlacing low hedges of coloured leaved shrubs, such as santolina and lavender, set in gravel, decorate a sheltered corner. *Below:* A sixteenth-century fountain adds its magic to the birdsong of a green peaceful enclosure. *Below right:* As decoration, the fashion in Tudor days was to embellish their gardens with heraldic animals set in high, parti-coloured poles.

In the reign of Henry VIII, the occupant of Tudor House (as it is now called) in Southampton, was a very grand personage indeed – the Lord Chief Justice of England, no less, Sir Richard Lyster. 'The scented, walled garden', suggests Sylvia Landsberg, who writes so tellingly about the recreation of this little jewel, must have been 'a refuge for him, from disease-ridden noisy London. Sitting in his garden arbour, Sir Richard would often have had much on his mind, including fear for his own head, as he mused on the successive deaths of those associated with Henry VIII'. Miss Landsberg pictures Lady Lyster's relationship to her garden, culling herbs to scent the house or distil potions: 'as the Lord's wife she was physician to the local poor'; she would have cared for her bees; perhaps trained the tail of a topiary peacock; and embroidered the ground with interlaced patterns of coloured-leaved herbs.

Some years ago it was decided to try to recreate the garden as it once could have looked during the period 1485-1603. There was not much to go on, but with enthusiasm, generosity and valuable advice, the Park Department of Southampton Leisure Services set about their task. This beautiful little garden, open to all to visit, free, is now there, in Bugle Street, Southampton, looking much as it must have looked when Sir Thomas More wrote, in 1519, how his contemporaries 'Set great store by their gardens: in them they have . . . all manner of fruit, herbs and flowers so pleasant, well furnished and fynely kept . . .'

Jenkyn Place

BENTLEY, HAMPSHIRE

MR AND MRS G. E. COKE

There has been a house, and probably a garden, on the site of Jenkyn Place for centuries. The Pilgrims' Way passed over what is now the front drive, and the house itself got its curious name from Janckne's Well, which is mentioned in Domesday Book, and still exists today.

Mr and Mrs Gerald Coke bought the place in 1941 – not a promising year for laying out pleasure grounds. It was not until two or three years after the war that they started serious work on the garden. The soil was ideal – upper green sand, in which most plants thrive, and which none dislikes. The situation – on the north side of the Wey Valley, facing south – was sheltered. There were good trees and old walls.

The garden was planned as a series of separate enclosures, of different sizes, and each with its own character. The garden's complex, though thoughtful, planning was evolved by the owners, with the aid of their admirable gardener and friend, Walter Sherfield.

Their joint aim was to conjure a garden which would be a beautiful setting for the house, and a place to walk in 'and find something to provide interest or delight' at most times of the year.

Some of the rarer and more interesting shrubs, trees and plants which will 'interest and delight' the visitor to the gardens include Schizandra grandiflora rubrifolia, the daisy flowered Mutisia ilicifolia, and Actinidia Kolomikta with its oddly coloured leaves, all of which can be found by the drive or in the forecourt.

In the Dutch garden, there are fine specimens of Ceanothus russelianus, the white-flowered Rosa Madame Plantier, with apple-green foliage, the seldom-met-with Dregea sinensis, a climbing shrub from China, and an impressive white Tree Peony Yano okima, as well as its exquisite, lower-growing relation, the butter-yellow Paeonia mlokosewitchii: Colletia armata rosea, sharp-spined and white-flowered, fills the air with its aroma in August, and eighteenth-century

The house, *opposite*, seen over a rose-clad wall of brick and local 'clunch'. *Above left*: Rough walls, smooth paving and an invasive, but always welcome Cotoneaster horizontalis. *Right*: An eighteenth-century marble Ganymede, after Giovanni Bologna.

tubs hold lemon-scented verbena. On the wall of the rose garden, besides roses, there flowers in June the rare Caesalpinia japonica, with spidery yellow flowers, and the equally unusual Buddleia colvilei, with flowers like pink grapes.

In the shrub borders there are a mass of interesting things, such as Callistemon linearis of the myrtle family; that elegant bamboo-like berberis, from Japan; Nandina domestica; the pea-flowered Ononis fruticosa; two miniature philadelphus, and useful plants for any gardeners with restricted garden room, Manteau d'Hermine and microphyllus. There is too little space to salute all the interesting plants in the herbaceous border at Jenkyn Place, but a rosy-leafed Photinia serrulata, near the gates, deserves special mention.

Other plants which add their own special beauty to the garden, at different times of the year, are magnificent magnolias, eleven different varieties of cotoneaster, Lonicera etrusca, which shows lemon-yellow flowers in July, Pterostyrax hispida from China, and the tender, heavily scented trachelospermum and mandevilla, two plants which the writer of this book first saw growing in India. Another noteworthy shrub is what many people consider to be the best of the abelias, the deciduous and large-flowered Abelia Schumannii.

The garden at Jenkyn Place is a place of beauty and fascination for many months of the year. It is a garden which should be high on the list of any lover of gardens, a garden to which any garden pilgrim would be wise to make his way.

T owering Eremurus bungei, *opposite*, rocketing upwards against a dusky background of evergreens. *Above*: Iris sibirica in early summer. *Left*: Pelargoniums and geraniums with scented leaves, grouped round a sundial. *Below*: Hybrid musk roses lay their sweetness on the air.

I only tell the sunny hours.

Most of the gardens in this book are occasionally
open to the public. For details see the 'Yellow Book',
published by the National Gardens Scheme, or
'Historic Houses, Castles and Gardens.' Both are on
sale at most bookshops, bookstalls or Tourist Centres.